Down the Yellowstone

Down the Yellowstone

By Lewis R. Freeman

Copyright

Contents

I - THE YELLOWSTONE IN WINTER

The present day Indian inhabitants of the Yellowstone and Big Horn valleys, whose ancestors hunted bear, buffalo and elk in the Devil's Land now known as Yellowstone Park, preserve a legend to the effect that when the world was made, because this region was the most desirable section of Creation, Mog the God of Fire, and Lob the God of rains and snows, contended for the control of it. After some preliminary skirmishing, the disputants carried the matter to the court of the Great Spirit for settlement. Here the ruling was that Mog should occupy the land for six moons, when Lob should follow with possession for a similar interval, thus dividing the year equally between them.

But Mog, being a bad god as well as a tricky one, spent his first six moons in connecting the valleys with hell by a thousand passages, and thus bringing up fire and sulphur and boiling water wherever it suited his fiendish fancy. Then he threw dust on all of the beautiful colored mountains, dried up the grass and shook the leaves from the trees, so that when it came to his rival's turn to take charge, Lob found affairs in a very sad way indeed.

But Lob set himself to work, like the good god that he was, and dusted and furbished up the mountains, watered the grass and trees, and heaped the snow in mighty drifts on geyser and hot spring in an effort to stop their mouths and force their boiling waters back from whence they came. But the latter task was too much for him. When the end of his allotted time came, though the grass was springing green and fresh and the trees were bursting into leaf again, the geysers and hot springs spouted merrily on. All the incoming Mog had to do was to kick up a few clouds of dust and turn the sun loose on the grass and trees to have the place just as he had left it.

And so for some thousands of alternating tenancies the fight has gone on, all the best of it with the bad god. Although Lob is gaining somewhat year by year, and has already dried many a spouting geyser and bubbling hot spring and reduced countless pots of boiling sulphur to beds of yellow crystals, he still has many a moon to work before he can force hell to receive its own and leave him free to complete his mighty task of reclamation.

In strong support of this legend is the fact that at the time of year when the Indians say that Lob is compelled to abdicate, and before Mog begins his annual dust-throwing—the middle of April or thereabouts,—the Yellowstone Park is incomparably more beautiful than at any other season. And moreover, there are those who maintain that even at other seasons it is still more beautiful than any other place in the world, just as it was in the beginning when it aroused the jealousies of the rival gods and precipitated their eternal conflict.

What the Yellowstone is in the early spring only those who have seen it at that season can realize, and only those who have made the summer tour are in a position to imagine. Let one who has breasted the sweltering heat-waves that radiate from Obsidian Cliff in July, trying to picture the impressive beauty of that massive pile of volcanic glass through the translucent dust-clouds raised by the passage of two or three score cars—let him fancy that cliff, its summit crowned with a feathered crest of snow, huge drifts at its base, and its whole face, washed and polished by the elements, glittering as though panelled with shining ebony. Let him think of the time his car was halted on the Continental Divide and the driver endeavoured to point out one of the distant eminences, guessed dimly through the smoke-clouds rising beyond Shoshone Lake, as the Grand Teton, and then fancy himself standing at the same point and looking out across the valley through air that, windowed and cleansed by the winds and snows of the winter, is so clear that the bottle-green in the rims of the glaciers is discernible at forty miles. Let him who has admired the transcendent beauty of the steam-clouds swirling above Old Faithful in the summer imagine these clouds increased two-fold in whiteness and density, and ten-fold in volume, by the quicker condensation of a zero morning. Let him picture the black gorge of the Fire Hole Canyon, where the river plunges down to the Upper Geyser Basin, forming Kepplar Cascade, transformed to a shining fairyland of sparkling crystal and silver, everything in range of the flying spray spangled and plated and jewelled by the ice and frost, as though a whole summer day's sunshine had been shaken up with a winter night's snowfall, and then fashioned by an army of elfin workmen into a marvellous million-pieced fretwork, adorned with traceries ethereal and delicate, and of a fragile loveliness beyond words to describe.

All these things, and many more, the summer tourist will have to picture in coming near to a conception of what the wizardry of winter has effected. There is the novelty of seeing a rim of ice around the Devil's Frying Pan, and the great hole that the up-shooting gush of a geyser tears in a cloud of driven snow. There is the massive beauty of the ice bulwark upon Virginia Cascade, and then, in winter as in summer the scenic climax, the lower falls and the Grand Canyon.

And nowhere more than in the incomparable Canyon is the general effect heightened by the presence of the ice and the snow and the clean-washed air. The very existence of the brilliant streaks and patches of yellow and umber and a dozen shades of red depends upon the water from the rain and melting snow dissolving the colouring matters from the rocks of the upper levels and depositing them upon the canyon walls as it trickles down to the river. Clear and sharp in the early springtime, the bright pigments are bleached and blended by the sun and winds of the summer until, by the time the fall storms set in, the contrast between streak and streak is far less marked than when, chrysalis like, they first burst from their snow cocoons of winter.

It is in the spring, when the blaze of the great colour-drenched diorama is set off by patches of dazzling snow, when every vagrant sunbeam glancing from the canyon side is caught and refracted in the mazes of glittering icicles that fringe every jutting cornice and battlement till it reaches the eyes of the beholder like a flash from a thousand-hued star; when the slide from the mountainside forms a snow dam in the river, and the angry torrent, leaping like a lion at the bars of its cage, brushes away the obstruction and rages onward in renewed fury to the valley; when the great mouth under the snow-cap at the top of the falls is tearing itself wider day by day in its frantic efforts to disgorge the swollen stream that comes surging down from the over-flowing lake— it is at this time, when Nature has whipped on her mightiest forces to the extreme limit of their powers in a grandstand finish to her spring house-cleaning, that the Grand Canyon of the Yellowstone has a beauty and a depth of appeal beyond all other seasons.

From the time that I first conceived the idea of an early springtime trip through the Yellowstone Park the difficulties in the way of carrying out such a plan, like rolled snowballs, seemed to grow as my inquiries progressed. Every objection was urged, from the possibility of snow-blindness to the certainty of death from cold, snow-slides, or wild animals, from the probability of opposition from the Fort to the improbability of securing provisions en route. Old "Yankee Jim" even told me that the spirits of the hot springs and geysers, while peaceable enough in the mild days of summer, were not to be trusted after they had been "riled and fruz" by the winds and snows of winter. That was about the last straw. I felt that I was literally between the devil and the deep snow.

But when I reached Fort Yellowstone, at the entrance to the Park, I learned that nearly the whole of the hundred and fifty miles of road followed on the summer tour were patrolled by soldiers, and that the scouts made a complete round several times during the winter. The officer in command received me most kindly. He had no objection at all to my going out with the scouts or the soldiers on game patrol. If I would satisfy him that I could conduct myself properly on ski he would see that all necessary equipment and facilities were provided me for the winter tour.

I learned later that the sergeant who was detailed to test me out had boasted that he intended to break me of my fool notion if he had to break my fool neck. From the way he started, I am actually inclined to believe he meant it. He led me on foot up the road to Golden Gate, circled round to the west, ordered me to put on my ski, and then started down through the timber toward the terraces of Mammoth Hot Springs. I, of course, fell at the end of ten feet. Having little way on, my worst difficulty was getting my head out from under the toe of my left ski the while that same toe was held down by the rear end of my right ski. It was just the usual ski beginner's mix-up. My instructor, however, had descended about five hundred feet right side up when a loop of willow caught the toe of one of his ski and sent him spinning the next five hundred end over end. It was only by the greatest of good luck that he kissed lightly off five or six trees in passing instead of colliding with one head-on. Even as it was they had to send a sled up from the fort to bring down his much-abused anatomy. The remainder of my ski novitiate, thank heaven, was served under the skilful and considerate tutelage of Peter Holt, the scout. Thanks to my Alaska snow-shoe work and the fact that I was hard as nails physically, I was pronounced ready to take the road at the end of a couple of days. It was intensive training, and accompanied by many bumps and thrills. I shall probably always be in Holt's debt for the bumps. Most of the thrills I paid back last June when, finding him the Chief of Police of Livingston, I took him along as passenger for the first fifty miles of my run down the Yellowstone.

The morning after I was adjudged sufficiently ski-broke to attempt the winter tour of the Park with a fair chance of finishing I was attached to a party of troopers detailed to pack in bacon to the station at Norris Basin. The memories of the doings of the delectable weeks that followed, which I spent with bear and elk and spouting geysers and bubbling mud springs as my daily play-fellows, are still tinged with rose at the end of a score of years. I am appending here—in the form of verbatim extracts from my religiously kept diary—some account of a few of the more amusing episodes. The wording follows hard upon the original; the spelling, I regret to say, I have just had to go over with a dictionary and dephonetize. If the view-point is a bit naïve in spots, please remember that you are reading the babblings of a very moony and immature youth, more or less tipsy with his first draughts of life, who had just discovered that he was standing on the verge of a world full of innumerable things and imagining that they were all put there for his own special entertainment.

Lake Station, April 13. Corporal Hope and I set out this morning from the Patrol Station, going after elk and buffalo pictures. Heading in the direction of Hayden Valley, we encountered two buffalo cows and their calves crossing a half-bare opening in the trees near the Mud Geyser. We had little difficulty in heading them as they tried to break away and driving them off on a course that offered me a favourable exposure. The calves were a month or more old, but tottered on their thin legs and seemed very weak, the consequence, no doubt, of continued inbreeding. The rapidly thinning herd is badly in need of an infusion of new blood.

We came upon the main herd farther down the valley, making some long-distance snap-shots on various individuals and sections of it as they went lunging off through the drifts at our approach. It was old "Tuskegee," reputed to be the largest specimen of the Bison Americanus in existence, whose picture I most cared for. The old fellow is estimated to weigh over 3000 pounds, is covered with a net-work of scars from his lifetime of fighting, and has only one eye and the remnant of a tail left. He has been seen to give battle to three pugnacious bull elk at once, and has killed numbers of them in single combat.

It was but a few summers ago that old "Tuskegee" left the herd, charged a coach full of tourists, goring one of the horses so badly that it had to be shot. The big vehicle was nearly overturned by the plunging horses, while its occupants—a party of New England school-teachers—were driven into frenzies of terror. Neither the bullets from a nickel-plated revolver in the hands of one of the schoolmarms, nor the long stinging whip of the driver, nor even his equally long and stinging oaths, affected "Tuskegee" in the least. He continued butting about among the frightened horses as though the wrecking of a six-in-hand coach was a regular part of his daily routine. At last, however, the sustained hysteria of the females seemed to get upon the old fellow's nerves. Wheeling about, he turned the stub of his tail to the swooning tourists and galloped, bellowing, over the hill.

An order was at once issued that "Tuskegee" should be shot on sight, and for a month a special detail from the Fort scoured the hills and valleys in search of the renegade. But all to no purpose. The old warrior, as though understanding that he was persona non grata with the authorities, retreated into the impenetrable fastnesses of the mountain spurs above Thorofare Plateau, and nothing was seen or heard of him for many months.

For two years there was an interregnum in buffalodom, during which the big herd gradually dropped to pieces and wandered about in leaderless fragments. Then, one day, a big bull elk was found, crushed and torn, trampled into the mud of Violet Springs, and the scouts told each other that the King had returned. A few days later a soldier of the game patrol, on a run through Hayden Valley, saw the reunited herd debouch from a canyon, with old "Tuskegee" puffing proudly in the lead. His tail was stubbier than ever, the grizzled red hair was more patchy on the rump and more matted on the neck, and a new set of scars was criss-crossed and etched into the old ones upon his flanks. The old fighting spirit still flamed, however, and the trooper owed his life to the fact that the snow was deep, the crust firm, the slope down and his ski well waxed. But a new superintendent was in charge, and his satisfaction at seeing the scattered herd once more united was so great that he stayed the order of execution. Since that time, strangely enough, "Tuskegee" has appeared to show his appreciation of this official clemency by behaving in a most exemplary manner.

I was endeavouring to get a picture of the main herd before it broke up, when Hope espied old "Stub Tail" in the rear of a bunch of young cows who were heading away for the hills. Shouting for me to join him, he gave chase. We gained on them easily in the heavy snow of the valley, and almost overtook them where they floundered, belly-deep, on their erratic course. Then they struck the wind-swept slopes of the lower hills, where the agile cows drew away from us rapidly and scampered out of sight. But not so old "Tuskegee." Whether it was rheumatism in his stiff old joints that made him stop, or simple weariness, or, as is most likely, the unconquerable pride that would not permit him to turn his back upon an enemy, I shall not attempt to say. In any case, he wheeled and faced us, head low, hoofs pawing the moss, and snorting in angry defiance.

As he stood with his rugged form towering against the white background of the snowy hillside, two jets of steam rushing from his nostrils, his jaws flecked with bloody foam, his one eye gleaming green as the starboard light of a steamer, and his bellows of rage so deep that they seemed to come from beneath the earth, old "Tuskegee" might have been the vindictive incarnation of the spirit of all the geysers and hell holes in the Yellowstone bent on an errand of wrath and destruction.

Right then and there I forgot what I came for, forgot the picture I had intended to take, forgot everything but that snorting colossus in front of me and the fact that the hillside sloped invitingly in the opposite direction. Wherefore I tried to swing around, and in swinging turned too short, crossed my ski, and fell in a heap with my face in the snow.

They say that an ostrich will snuggle its head contentedly into the sand and let a band of Arabs with drawn scimitars charge right into its tail feathers. This may be quite true. Perhaps the climate of the Sahara has something to do with it. But it won't work with a man, a bull buffalo and a snowdrift, particularly if the man is strapped to two ten-foot-six strips of hickory and the bull buffalo has a bad reputation.

The faith, folly, foolishness, or whatever it is of the ostrich would have saved me a lot of unpleasant apprehensions. Every moment of the time I struggled to unsocket my head from under the nose of one of my ski I was sure I was going to be gored the next. And I am certain I was down all of five minutes, notwithstanding Hope's assertion that he had me straightened out and on my feet inside of ten seconds.

"Steady, young feller," I heard him saying as I rubbed the snow from my eyes; "don't lose your head like that again." (I wonder if he meant that literally.) "Old 'Tusky' won't hurt a fly nowadays. He's just posing for his picture. Gimme that camera. Hold up there; tain't nothing to be scared of!

That last was shouted at me as I gave a push with my pole and began to slide off down the hill out of the danger zone. Swinging round to a reluctant standstill, I meekly unslung my camera as Hope came down for it. Then, all set for a start, I watched him as he zigzagged back up the hill toward the buffalo. "Tusky" was blowing like a young Vesuvius, but the nervy fellow, not a whit daunted, edged up to within twenty feet of the steaming monster, waited calmly for the sun to come out from behind a cloud, and snapped the camera. Then we coasted back to the valley—I well in the lead,—leaving the resolute old monster in full possession of the field.

Our chase of the fleet-footed wapita was attended by less excitement but more exertion than was our pursuit of the bison. Following a trail from Violet Springs, we were lucky in encountering a herd of from four to five hundred grazing where the spring sunshine was uncovering the grass on a broad expanse of southerly sloping upland. We circled to the higher hills in an endeavour to drive a portion of the herd to the deeper snow of the valley, where we could overtake them on our ski. In the course of our climb we came upon a fine young bull of two years or thereabouts, lying in an alder thicket badly wounded from fighting. One of his graceful horns was snapped squarely off a foot from the head, his sides were frightfully bruised and torn, and so weak was he from loss of blood that he took no notice whatever of our approach. Hope said that few bulls are killed outright in their fights, but that most of the badly wounded ones ultimately die from "scab."

Our efforts to turn the elk to the valley was only partially successful, for the main herd, as though divining our purpose, set off on a mad stampede for the mountains, and on a course which made it impossible to head them. Hope, however, at imminent risk of his neck, dropped like a meteor over the rim of the mesa, negotiated a precarious serpentine curve among the butts of a lot of deadfalls, and just succeeded in cutting off a large bunch of cows, half a dozen "spike" bulls, and a fine old fourteen-pointer.

The bulls were brave enough at the beginning of the chase, where the snow was light and the going easy. The old fellow in particular kept well to the rear of his flying family, stopping every now and then to brandish his horns and give voice to clear, penetrating cries of defiance and anger. But as the herd wallowed into the coulée that skirted the foot of the hills his courage deserted him. He, in turn, deserted his family, and it was sauve qui peut for the lot of them. By the time our glistening hickories pulled us up on the flank of the bunch of heaving, sobbing cows, old "Fourteen Points" was a good hundred yards ahead, with the "spikes" scattered in between.

We easily headed the frightened cows as they floundered shoulder-deep, and I snapped them several times without much trouble. Then we turned our attention to the big bull. He, in his terror, had charged straight on down the coulée, going into increasingly deep snow at every bound. His efforts were magnificent to behold. At times only the tips of his shining antlers were visible; again, he would break through with his fore feet and fall with his muzzle in the snow, only his hind quarters showing above the crust. At times he would be down fore and aft, disappearing completely from sight, only the sound of his mighty limbs as they churned the honey-combed snow telling the story of the struggle.

His agility was wonderful. Every ounce of bone, every shred of muscle, every fiber of nerve was strained to its utmost. Time and again I saw his rear hoofs drawn as far forward and as high as his shoulders in an effort to gain a solid footing. When the hold of his hind legs was lost he would reach out and bury his fore hoofs and nose in the sinking crust, and then, arching his back, try to drag his great body up to them.

As we pulled up close behind him he wallowed into the shadow of some tall pines where the crust, unexposed to the sun, was hard and firm. He struggled to the surface, tottered across the shadowed space and began to break through on the farther side. Backing up, he tried a fresh place, but only to break through with all fours. Finally, all his former courage seeming to return with a rush, he staggered back against a tree, lowered his head, and with a shrill trumpet of defiance dared us to come on.

That was just what we had hoped and planned for. Circling on the soft snow, well beyond the reach of a rush, I made several snaps before we coasted away and left him free to return to his family and explain his desertion as best he might. The grating of his teeth, as he ground them together in elk-ish fury, followed us for some distance as we slid away down the coulée.

My attempt to secure some mountain sheep pictures by following the same methods employed with the bison and elk was brought to a sudden termination by what came so near to proving a serious disaster to the quarry that it quite destroyed my zest for the new sport and made me decide with regret to give it up as incompatible with my career as a writer on game protection. This occurred on the mountains above the Gardiner River not long after I had returned to Mammoth Hot Springs from my circular tour on ski. Hope, whose time in the Army was about up, was my fellow culprit. Both of us doubtless deserved to be clapped in the guard-house, as we surely would have been had the true account of what happened come out at the time. Now, at the end of twenty years, probably it won't matter a lot. Certainly not to Hope in any event. After serving out three or four more re-enlistments, he was killed in the Argonne in one of the last actions of the war. I quote again from my diary.

Mammoth Hot Springs, April 23.

Hope and I came within a hair of wiping out the cream of the Yellowstone Park herd of Ovis Montana this morning while trying to take its picture. I took the picture all right, but as a consequence of it the herd took a header into the river. I think all of them got out, but it was a narrow squeeze at the best. If there is ever an official inquiry into our operations, I am afraid my reputation as a game protector will be gone beyond all hope. This was the way the thing happened:

We had located with our glasses a large flock of fine animals several hundred yards below our lookout on Gardiner Mountain. Hope set off along the ridge to the windward of them, holding their interest so successfully in that direction that I was able to coast down from the opposite side and bring up almost in their midst before one of them knew what had happened. I had time for one hurried snap before they were off, and another when a swift quarter-mile coast brought me up almost on the heels of the vanguard of the flying flock.

Down a couple of hundred yards of easy slope I held even with the tail of the flock, and was manœuvring for another exposure when they came out upon a stretch of almost level bench above the river and began to beat me three-to-one. The leaders had all but reached the shelter of the timber when Hope, brandishing his pole and whooping like a wild Indian, dropped with the suddenness of a thunderbolt from somewhere among the snowy cliffs above and turned them back. The unexpected appearance of a new enemy sent glimmering such wits as the grizzled old leader still had. With one frightened glance to where I came labouring down on him from the rear, he turned and went plunging over the rim of the cliff onto the honey-combed ice and snow that bridged the river torrent, the whole flock following in his wake.

Hope, wide eyed with consternation, was peering over the edge of the cliff as I came up, and together we watched the various members of the flock pull themselves together, flounder through to the opposite bank and make off into the alder thicket beyond. The game struggle of the old patriarch was splendid. The first to leap, his unfortunate anatomy, half buried in the yielding snow, had received the impact of more than a few of the flying hoofs and horns that followed. For four or five long minutes after the last of his mates had struggled through to safety he lay, stunned and bleeding, on a slender peninsula of firm snow that jutted out over the surging stream. As the sound of our voices, loud and tense with guilty anxiety, floated down to him, he roused, pulled himself together, and at almost the first flounder broke through and went whirling off in the clutch of the angry current.

At the lower end of the cave-in his high-flung horns caught against the rim of soft ice, giving him a brief, but what we felt sure could be no more than a temporary, respite from an apparently certain fate. But we underrated the mettle of the brave old veteran, for even while his sturdy hind quarters drew down in the grip of the powerful undercurrent, one sharp fore hoof after the other gained hold on the trembling crust, and his sinewy body was almost lifted to safety before the sagging mass gave way again and left him struggling in the water. Twice, and then once again, was this same plucky manœuvre repeated, but only to end each time in the same heart-breaking failure. Every fibre of rippling muscle seemed strained to the limit in his final effort, and when the soggy ice broke away it looked certain that the river was to be the victor after all.

And such, no doubt, would have been the end had not the last cave-in carried the resolute old patriarch to a submerged bar of shingle. Here, rallying his seemingly inexhaustible strength, he gathered himself and leaped cleanly to a solid stretch of crust. A moment later he was off in the wake of the rest of his flock.

With long-drawn breaths of relief we turned and tightened up the thongs of our ski for the climb out of the canyon. It was not until half an hour later, when we paused for rest on the mesa rim, that Hope's drawling voice broke the silence that had held between us.

"Young feller," he said jerkedly between breaths, "if the old one had drownded down there, the best thing you and I could do would be to jump in and be drownded with him. Even as it is, if the Super gets wind of that monkey show, it's me for a disonerable discharge and you for over the border."

But as neither Hope nor I is inclined to do any talking, the chances seem good that we'll steer clear of the trouble we were so surely asking for. But no more ski-snapping for me, just the same.

The steamer *Expansion* on the Yellowstone, 1907

III - HIGH LIGHTS AND LOW LIGHTS

Grand Canyon Station, April 9.

We made a three o'clock start from Norris this morning and came all the way to the Canyon on the crust. Carr, one of the troopers accompanying me, took a fearful tumble on the winding hill that leads down to the Devil's Elbow, breaking his "gee-pole" and badly wrenching one of his ankles. A fierce thunder-storm overtook us about seven. The vivid flashes of the lightning produced a most striking effect in illuminating the inky clouds as they were blown across the snowy peaks. A flock of mountain sheep, driven from the upper spurs by the fury of the storm, crossed close to the road. I snapped a very unusual silhouette of them as they paused on the crest of a hill, with the blown storm-clouds in the background.

We reached the hotel before the storm was over. Bursting into the rear entrance, we were just in time to find Clark, the winter keeper, picking himself up from the middle of the floor, where he had been thrown after coming in contact with an electric current brought in on the telephone wire while he was tinkering with the receiver. The chap seems to be an inventive genius. He has, so the soldiers told me, dissected over a dozen clocks in an effort to secure the machinery for a model of an automobile sled he is working on. His last model was destroyed by his dog, which took the strangely acting thing for a bird or a rat and shook it to pieces before any one could interfere. A few days later the brute essayed to follow Clark on one of his wild slides down the side of the canyon to the brink of the falls, but lost his footing and went over into the scenery. The inventor considers this a propitious sign from heaven.

"For why should that dog go over the very first time he tried the slide after he did that destruction," he asked us, "if it wasn't because the Lord thought he stood in the way of good work? Now, with nothing to bother me, I shall build another model and reap my reward."

"But was the dog your only obstacle?" I asked.

"By no means," was the reply; "but all the others will be brushed away just as was the dog."

Hearken to that, oh ye of little faith! If faith will move mountains there surely ought to be no trouble about the movement of Clark's automobile sled.

Clark took me down the sidling snow-choked trail to the top of the falls this afternoon, saying that he wanted to show me how he did his famous "Devil's Slide." Utterly unable, in my comparative inexperience, to keep the road, I was about to beg off when Clark suggested that I remove my ski and ride the rest of the way by standing on the back of his. It was a hair-raising coast, but we made the brink without a spill. More important still—a point respecting which I had been most in doubt,—we stopped there.

Already considerably shaken in nerve, I tried to dissuade Clark from attempting his slide. Replying that the stunt was a part of his daily routine for keeping his wits on edge, he "corduroyed" off up the side of the canyon, which at that point has a slope of about forty-five degrees. When he was perhaps a hundred feet above my head, he laid hold of a sapling, swung quickly around, and shot full-tilt for the icy brink. I was sure he intended to kill himself, just as so many cracked inventors do. A sudden numbness seized me. The roar of the fall grew deafening, and I involuntarily closed my eyes. There was a thud and a crash, a shower of fine snow flew over me. Then the roar of the fall resumed.

When I mustered up the courage to open my eyes, it was to discover my mad companion cautiously drawing himself back from the brink. He had stopped, as usual, by throwing himself on his side and digging the edges of his ski into the frozen snow. Although he wouldn't admit it, I am certain he kept going an inch or two more than was his wont, for one long strip of hickory was swinging free beyond the icy edge and the other held by only a thin ridge of hard snow.

While he was still thus poised on the brink of Kingdom Come, or rather the Falls of the Yellowstone, Clark insisted on explaining to me the principle of a parachute cape he had devised for use in such an emergency. He reckoned that it would not only help in checking his momentum at the proper moment, but would also have a tendency to make his landing much less painful in the event he went over. I am wondering tonight if all inventors are like that. Clark is the first genius I have ever known, so I can't be quite sure.

Grand Canyon Station, April 10.

Clark and Smith took me out for a ski-jumping lesson this morning. Clark seems to be rather a star performer in all departments of ski work, but he claims that he is better at jumping than at anything else. What the long, straight drive, hit cleanly from the tee, is to the golfer, what the five rails, fairly taken, is to the cross-country rider, what the dash down a rocky-walled canyon is to the river boatman, the jump is to the ski-runner. But what the foozle is to the golfer, the cropper to the rider, the spill in midstream to the boatman, the fall at the end of the jump is to the ski-man. I saw both the jump and the fall today. Or rather, I saw the jump and felt the fall. If I saw anything at all, it was stars.

The jump is made from a raised "take-off" at the foot of a hill. The steeper the hill the better. The snow slopes up from the foot of the hill to the brink of the "take-off," where it ends abruptly. The jumper goes off up the hill for a quarter of a mile or so, turns round and coasts down at full speed. Leaving the "take-off" at a mile or more a minute, it is inevitable that he must be shot a considerable distance through the air. If he is well balanced at the proper moment he naturally sails a lot farther than if he is floundering and Dutch-windmilling with his arms. Also, he messes himself and the snow up a lot less when he lands.

Considering their short runway and crudely built "take-off," the sixty feet Clark cleared this morning was a fairly creditable performance, though probably less than half what some of the cracks do in Norway. Naturally, I could hardly be expected to do as well as that. It was only on the last of a dozen trials that I managed to coast all the way to the brink of the "take-off" without falling, and even then I was not sufficiently under control to stream-line properly and so minimize air resistance. Under the circumstances, therefore, I am rather pleased with Clark's verdict anent my maiden effort. He said I hit harder and showed less damage from it than any man in the Park.

Grand Canyon Station, April 11.

This morning we went down to Inspiration Point to watch the sunrise. Never before did I realize how inadequate the most pretentious descriptions of the Grand Canyon of the Yellowstone all are. The greatest of the world's word painters have only succeeded in stringing together a lot of colours like the variegated tags on a paint company's sample sheet, throwing in a liberal supply of trope and hyperbole, making a few comparisons to heaven and hell, sunrise and sunset and a field of flowers, and mixing the whole together and serving it up garnished with adjectives of the awful, terrible, immense and stupendous order.

It is not in singling out each crag and pinnacle, or in separating each bright streak of colour from its neighbour and admiring it alone, that one comes to the fullest appreciation of the grandeur and beauty of the canyon. It is rather in being gradually taken possession of by the spirit of the place, an influence that lasts long after you have ceased to look, a feeling far deeper than the mere transient delight of gazing on a beautiful picture.

Yesterday's thaw must have raised the water in the Lake. The river is much higher today, and the snow-bridges above the falls, as well as the heaped-in drifts below, are breaking away in huge masses. The snow-cap on the brink, with the water gushing forth from under it, has much the appearance of a gigantic alabaster gargoyle. The river shoots down under the snow and leaps out over the chasm in a clean compact stream of bottle-green. Half-way down the resistance of the air has whitened the jet, and as it disappears behind the great pile at its foot it is dashed to a spray so snowy that, from a distance, the line between water and drift defies the eye to fix.

Lake Station, April 12.

As we edged our way out to a better position the sun rose and threw a series of three rainbows in the mist clouds as they floated up out of the shadowed depths. The lowest and clearest of these semi-circles of irised spray seemed to spring from a patch of bright saffron sand, where it was laid bare by the melting snow. Now I know where the story of the gold at the end of the rainbow came from.

Carr and I tried to come through from the Canyon by moonlight last night and had rather a bad time of it. First a fog obscured the moon. Then we tried to take a short cut by following the telephone line, got lost in the dark, and staid lost till the moon set and made it darker still. In cutting across the hills to get back into Hayden Valley, Carr fell over a snow-bank and landed right in the middle of the road, where it had been laid bare by the heat of hot springs. Starting again, we came to the top of a hill and coasted down at a smart gait. As we sped to the bottom I became aware of a dark blur beyond the white of the snow. Then there was a sudden stoppage, and I seemed to see a re-risen moon, with a whole cortège of comets in its wake, dancing about the sky. I came to at the touch of a handful of snow on my face, to learn that I had coasted right onto a bare spot in the road and stopped in half a ski-length. My heavily loaded knapsack, shooting along the line of least resistance up my spine, had come into violent contact with the back of my head, producing the astronomical pyrotechnic illusion.

After a while we were lost again, this time in a level space bounded on four sides by a winding creek. I know it was on four sides of the place, for we carefully walked off toward each point of the compass in rotation, and each time landed in the creek. We finally escaped by wading. How we got in without wading will always be a mystery. Carr said the stream was called Trout Creek. Doubtless he is right; but if there were any trout over six inches long there last night they must have been permanently disjointed at more than one vertebral connection by having to conform to those confounded bends.

We passed the famous and only Mud Geyser an hour before daybreak. Things were in a bad way with him, judging from the noise. The mutterings of the old mud-slinger in his quieter moments reminds me very much of a Chilkat Mission Indian reciting the Lord's Prayer in his native tongue—just a rapid succession of deep gutturals. But when some particularly indigestible concoction—served, possibly by subterranean dumb-waiter from the adjacent Devil's Kitchen—interferes with the gastronomies of the old epicure, his voice is anything but prayerful. Carr said it reminded him of something between a mad bull buffalo and a boat load of seasick tourists when the summer wind stirs up the Lake. But Carr was too tired and disgusted to be elegant. Indeed, we were both pretty well played out. Personally, I felt just about like the Mud Geyser sounded.

After about an hour's groping in the dark, we found an emergency cabin near the Mud Geyser. Building a fire, we warmed and ate a can of salmon. When it was light enough to see, we slipped on the ski and came through on the crust in short order.

Thumb Emergency Cabin, April 15.

Making a start before daybreak, we crossed Yellowstone Lake on the ice. It was a wonderful opportunity to watch the light and shade effects on the encircling mountains. Far to the south-west there is a very striking pyramidal peak. Two flat snow-paved slopes of the mighty pile, divided by an even ridge of black rock that rears itself in sharp contrast to the beds of white that bulwark the base, form the sides of the pyramid. The southeastern side so lies that it catches the first rays of the morning sun and sends them off in shimmering streamers across the lake—Nature's heliographic signal of the coming day.

An hour or more later the sun itself appears above the eastern hills, silvering the tops of the frosted fir trees and whitening the vaporous clouds above Steamboat Point and Brimstone Basin. The green ice in the little glaciers near the summit of the big mountain kindle and sparkle like handfuls of emeralds, and the reflected sun-flashes play in quivering motes of dancing light on the snowy flanks of Elephant Back.

Meanwhile the south-west face of the great pyramid, lying in heavy shadow, sleeps dull and black until the morning is well advanced. Then, suddenly, without a perceptible premonitory fading of the shadow plane, the whole snow-field becomes a shining sheet, as white and clear-cut as thought carved from alabaster. At noon the sun, standing full above the black dividing line of rock, sheds an impartial light on either side of the mountain. Perspective is lost for the moment, and there appears to be but one broad field of snow, with a black line traced down its middle.

Toward midafternoon the eastern side draws on its coat of black as suddenly as that of the other was cast aside in the morning. Now the former is almost indiscernible, while the latter, gleaming in the sunlight like a great sheet of white paper, seems suspended in the air by invisible wires. And there it continues to hang, while the shadows deepen along the shores and creep out over the ice in wavering lines as night descends upon the frozen lake. Gradually the white sheet fades to nothingness, until at last its position is marked only by a blank blur unpricked by the twinkle of awakening stars.

It is as though the page of the day, new, bright, pure and unsullied in the morning, had at last been turned to the place reserved for it from the dawn of creation, blackened and blemished and stained by the sins of a world of men.

(1922—I am considerably moved—I won't say how or to what—by that little "sins-of-a-world-of-men" touch. It is something to have begun life as a moralist, anyhow.)

Fountain Station, April 17.

This morning it was colder again, and we were witness of a most wonderful sight when a snow squall chanced along while the Fountain Geyser was in full eruption. The storm swooped down with sudden fury while we were watching the steam jets in the Mammoth Paint Pot throw evanescent lilies and roses in the coloured mud. We were waiting for the Great Fountain, most beautiful of all the geysers of the Park, to get over her fit of coyness and burst into action. The Fountain, by the way, is one of the few geysers always spoken of in the feminine gender. I asked if this was on account of her beauty, but Carr, who had a wife once, thinks her uncertainty of temper had more to do with it.

The imperious advance of the Storm King seemed still further to intimidate the bashful beauty, and at first she only shrank the deeper into her subterranean bower. But when the little snowflakes, like gentle but persistent caresses, began to shower softly upon the bosom of the pool the silver bubbles came surging up with a rush. In a moment more, as a maid overcome with the fervour of her love springs to the arms of her lover, the queenly geyser leaped forth in all her splendour, eight feet of beaming, bubbling green and white thrown with precipitate eagerness upon the bosom of the Storm King. Whereupon the latter threw all restraint to the winds and responded with a gust of bold, blustering, ungovernable passion. Roaring in his triumph, beating and winding her in sheets of driven snow, he grappled her in his might and bent her back and down until the great steam-clouds from her crest, like coils of flowing hair, were blown in curling masses along the earth.

For a full half hour they struggled in reckless abandon, granting full play to the ardour of their elemental passions, reeling and swaying in advance and retreat, as the mighty forces controlling them alternated in mastery. When the gusts fell light the geyser played to her full height, melting a wide circle in the snow that had been driven up to her very mouth. When the wind came again she bent, quivering to his will, but only to spring back erect as the gust weakened and died down.

Presently the storm passed, the sun came out and the north wind ceased to blow. Full of the gladness of her love, the queenly geyser reared, rippling, to her full height, held for a moment, a coruscating tower of brilliants, and then, with little sobs and gasps of happiness and contentment, sank back into her crystal chamber to dream and await the next coming of her impetuous northern lover. Or so I fancied, at any rate, as we watched the water sink away into the beryline depths of its crater. But I failed to reckon with the sex of the beauty. This afternoon, returning from a visit to Fairy Falls, we passed over the formation. An indolent young breeze, just awakened from his siesta among the southern hills, came picking his way up the valley of the Madison, and the fickle Fountain was fairly choking in her eagerness to tell how glad she was to see him. But her faithlessness had its proper reward. The blasé blade passed the flirtatious jade by without deigning even to ruffle her steam-cloud hair. The soldiers said he had probably gone on to keep an engagement at the Punch Bowl, where he has been in the habit of stirring things up a bit with a giddy young zephyr who blows in to meet him there from down Snake River way.

Norris Station, April 18.

This has been a memorable day, for in the course of it I have seen two of the most famous manifestations of the Yellowstone in action— the Giant Geyser erupting and Bill Wade swearing. The Giant is the biggest geyser in America, and Bill Wade is reputed to have the largest vocabulary of one-language profanity in the North-west. True, there is said to be a chap over in the legislature at Helena that can out-cuss Wade under certain conditions, but he is college bred, speaks four languages and has to be under the influence of liquor to do consistent work. Wade requires no artificial stimulants, but he does have to get mad before he can do himself full justice. Today something happened to make him sizzling mad. The eruption of the Giant is startling and beautiful, the river, as it takes its three-hundred-foot leap to the depths of the Grand Canyon, is sublime and awe-inspiring, but for sheer fearsomeness Wade's swearing—viewed dispassionately and with no consideration of its ethical bearing—is the real wonder of the Yellowstone.

We were climbing the hill back of the Fountain Hotel—Wade, two troopers and myself. Wade, who is the winter keeper of the hotel and not too skilled with ski, tried to push straight up the steep slope. Halfway to the top he slipped, fell over a stump, gained fresh impetus and came bounding to the bottom over the hard crust, a wildly waving pinwheel of arms, legs and clattering ski. He was torn, bruised and scratched from the brush and trees, and one of his long "hickories" was snapped at the instep. For the moment he uttered no word, but the soldiers, who knew what was coming, held their breath and waited in trembling anticipation. The air was charged as before a thunderstorm. A hush fell upon us all, a hush like the silence that settles upon a ring of tourists around Old Faithful as the boiling water, sinking back with gurgling growls, heralds the imminent eruption.

Wade removed his ski, laid the fragments on the snow and folded his coat across them, as a pious Mussulman spreads his prayer-mat. Seating himself cross-legged on the coat, he cast his eyes heavenward, on his face an expression as pure and passionless as that on the countenance of the Sistine Madonna. For a few moments he was silent, as though putting away earthly things and concentrating his mind on the business in hand. Then he began to summon the powers of heaven and the powers of hell and call them to reckoning. He held them all accountable. Then came the saints—every illustrious one in the calendar. Saint by saint he called them and bade them witness the state they had brought him to. Spirits of light, imps of darkness—all were charged in turn.

His voice grew shriller and shriller as his pent-up fury was unleashed. He cursed snow, hill, snags, stumps, trees and ski. He cursed by the eyes, as the sailor curses, and by the female progenitor, as the cowboy. He cursed till his face turned from white to red, from red to purple, from purple to black; he cursed till the veins in knots and cords seemed bursting from his forehead; he cursed till his voice sunk from a bellow to a raucous howl, weakened to convulsive gasps and died rattling in his throat, till brain and body reeled under the strain and he sank into a quivering heap at our feet.

I shall always regret that the eruption of the Park's greatest geyser came after, rather than before, that of Wade. Frankly, the spouting of the mighty Giant seemed a bit tame after the forces we had just seen unleashed over behind the hotel.

Wade, coming through to Norris with us this afternoon, got into more trouble. Unfortunately, too, it was under conditions which made it impracticable to relieve his feelings in a swear-fest. The snow around the Fountain was nearly all gone when we started, and we found it only in patches along the road down to the Madison. After carrying our ski for a mile without being able to use them, we decided on Holt's advice, to take the old wood trail over the hills. This, though rough and steep, was well covered with snow. We all took a good many tumbles in dodging trees and scrambling through the brush, Wade being particularly unfortunate. Finally, however, we reached the top of the long winding hill that leads back to the main road by the Gibbon River. Here we stopped to get our wind and tighten our ski-thongs for the downward plunge. At this point we discovered that the snow of the old road had been much broken and wallowed by some large animals.

"Grizzlies," pronounced Holt, as he examined the first of a long row of tracks that led off down the hill. "Do you see those claw marks? Nothing like a grizzly for nailing down his footprints. Doesn't seem to care if you do track him home."

The last words were almost lost as he disappeared, a grey streak, around the first bend. Carr and I hastened to follow, and Wade, awkwardly astride of his pole, brought up the rear. I rounded the turn at a sharp clip, cutting hard on the inside with my pole to keep the trail. Then, swinging into the straight stretch beyond, I waved my pole on high in the approved manner of real ski cracks, and gathered my breath for the downward plunge. And not until the air was beginning to whip my face and my speed was quite beyond control, did I see two great hairy beasts standing up to their shoulders in a hole in the middle of the trail. Holt was on them even as I looked. Holding his course until he all but reached the wallow, he swerved sharply to the right against the steeply sloping bank, passed the bears, and then eased back to the trail again. A few seconds later he was a twinkling shadow, flitting down the long lane of spruces in the river bottom.

The stolid brutes never moved from their tracks. I made no endeavour to stop, but, adopting Holt's tactics, managed to give a clumsy imitation of his superlatively clever avoidance of the blockade.

Venturing to glance back over my shoulder as I regained the trail, I crossed the points of my ski and was thrown headlong onto the crust. Beyond filling my eyes with snow I was not hurt in the least. My ski thongs were not even broken.

My momentary glance had revealed Wade, eyes popping from his head and face purple with frantic effort, riding his pole and straining every muscle to come to a stop. But all in vain. While I still struggled to get up and under way again, there came a crash and a yell from above, followed by a scuffle and a gust of snorts and snarls. When I regained my feet a few seconds later nothing was visible on the trail but the ends of two long strips of hickory. Scrambling up the side of the cut and falling over each other in their haste, went two panic stricken grizzlies.

Wade kicked out of his ski, crawled up from the hole, and was just about to spread his swear-mat and tell everything and everybody between high heaven and low hell what he thought of them for the trick they had played on him when, with a rumbling, quizzical growl, a huge hairy Jack-in-the-Box shot forth from a deep hole on the lower side of the road. Burrowing deep for succulent roots sweet with the first run of spring sap, the biggest grizzly of the lot had escaped the notice of both of us until he reared up on his haunches in an effort to learn what all the racket was about. A push with my pole quickly put me beyond reach of all possible complications. Poor Wade rolled and floundered for a hundred yards through the deep snow before stopping long enough to look back and observe that the third grizzly was beating him three-to-one—in the opposite direction. So profound was his relief that he seemed to forget all about the swear-fest. My companions claim they never knew anything of the kind to happen before.

Norris Station, April 19.

There are a number of things that are forbidden in Yellowstone Park, but the worst one a man can do, short of first degree murder, is to "soap" a geyser. Because the unnatural activity thus brought about is more than likely to result in the destruction of a geyser's digestive system, this offence—and most properly so—is very heavily penalized. Wherefore we are speculating tonight as to what will happen to little

Ikey Einstein in case the Superintendent finds out what he did this afternoon.

Ikey has had nothing to do with my tour at any time. That is one thing to be thankful for. Discharged from the Army a few days ago, he had been given some kind of job at the Lake Hotel for the summer. He is on his way there now, he says, and is holding over here for the crust to freeze before pushing on. Time was hanging rather heavily on his hands this afternoon, which is probably the reason that he cooked up a case of laundry soap in a five-gallon oil can and poured the resultant mess down the crater of "The Minute Man." The latter won its name as a consequence of playing with remarkable regularity practically upon the sixtieth tick of the minute from its last spout. Or, at least, that was what was claimed for it. Ikey maintains that he clocked it for half an hour, and that it never did better than once in eighty seconds, and that it was increasing its interval as the sun declined. He held that a geyser that refused to recognize its duty to live up to its name and reputation should be disciplined—just like in the Army. Perhaps it was discouraged from getting so far behind schedule. If that was the case, plainly the proper thing to do was to help it to make up lost time in one whale of an eruption, and then it might start with a clean slate and live up to its name. He was only acting for the geyser's own good. Thus Ikey, but only after he had put his theory into practice.

Ikey waited until he had the station to himself before cooking up his dope. Holt had pushed on to Mammoth Hot Springs and Carr and I had gone out to watch for the eruption of the Monarch. With no scout and non-com present, he doubtless figured he would run small chance of having his experiment interfered with. Carr and I, sitting on the formation over by the crater of the Monarch, saw him come down with an oil can on his shoulder and start fussing round in the vicinity of "The Minute Man." Suddenly a series of heavy reverberations shook the formation beneath our feet, and at the same instant Ikey turned tail and started to run. He was just in time to avoid the deluge from a great gush of water and steam that shot a hundred feet in the air, but not to escape the mountainous discharge of soapsuds that followed in its wake. Within a few seconds that original five gallons of soft soap had been beaten to a million times its original volume, and for a hundred yards to windward it covered the formation in great white, fluffy, iridescent heaps. Pear's Soap's original "Bubbles" boy wasn't a patch on the sputtering little Hebrew who finally pawed his way to fresh air and sunshine from the outermost of the sparkling saponaceous hillocks. Carr, whose mother had been a washer-woman, almost wept at the visions of his innocent childhood conjured up by the sight of such seas of suds.

For a good half hour "The Minute Man" retched and coughed in desperate efforts to spew forth the nauseous mess that had been poured down its throat. Then its efforts became scattering and spasmodic, finally ceasing entirely. For an hour longer a diminuendo of gasps and gurgles rattled in its racked throat. At last even these ceased, and a death-bed silence fell upon the formation. There has not been the flutter of a pulse since. It really looks as though "The Minute Man," his innermost vitals torn asunder by the terrific expansion of boiling water acting upon soft soap, is dead for good and all. I only hope I am not going to be mixed up in the inquest.

Crystal Springs Emergency Cabin, April 20.

Wade and I had a long and heated session of religious argument at Norris last night, of which I am inclined to think I had a shade the best. A half hour ago, however, he pulled off a coup which he seems to feel has about evened the score. At least I just overheard him telling Carr that, while that "dern'd reporter was a mighty slippery cuss," he reckoned that he finally got the pesky dude where he didn't have nothing more to say. This was something the way of it:

Wade is a sort of amateur agnostic, and, next to swearing, his favourite pastime is arguing "agin the church." He has read Voltaire and Bob Ingersoll in a haphazard way, and also sopped up some queer odds and ends from works on metaphysics and philosophy. These give him his basic ideas which, alchemized in the wonderworking laboratory of his mind, produce some golden theories. He holds, for instance, that no wise and beneficent being would cast a devil out of a woman and into a drove of hogs, because hogs were good to eat and women wasn't. Making the hogs run off a cut-bank into the sea meant spoiling good meat, and no wise and beneficent being would do that. He reckoned the whole yarn was just a bit of bull anyhow, and if it really did happen, wasn't modern science able to account for it by the fact that the girl was plain daffy and the hogs had "trichiny" worms and stampeded?

Little touches like that go a long way toward brightening the gloom of a winter evening, and for that reason I have done what I could to keep Wade on production. Unfortunately, my knowledge of theology is not profound, while Wade, with his wits sharpened on every itinerant sky-pilot who has ever endeavoured to herd in the black sheep of the Yellowstone, has all his guns ready to bear at a moment's notice. Naturally, therefore, in a matter of straight argument, he has had me on the run from his opening salvo. But always at the last I have robbed his victories of all sweetness by ducking back into the citadel of dogma, and telling him that I can't consent to argue with him unless he sticks to premises—that the Church cannot eliminate the element of faith, which he persists in ignoring. Then, leaving him fuming, I turn in and muffle my exposed ear with a pillow.

That was about the way it went last night at Norris, except that both of us, very childishly, lost our tempers and indulged in personalities. Wade refused to accept the fact of my retirement and violated my rest by staying up and poking the stove. When I uncovered my head to protest, he took the occasion to ask me how I reconciled the theory of the "conservashun" of matter with the story of the loaves and the fishes. I snapped out pettishly that I could reconcile myself to the story of the loaves and fishes a darn site easier than I could to the stories of a fish and a loafer. It was a shameful and inexcusable lapse of breeding on my part, especially as Wade, being a hotel watchman without active duties, was abnormally sensitive about being referred to as a loafer. At first he seemed to be divided between rushing me with a poker and sitting down for a swear-fest. Finally, however, he did a much more dignified thing than either by serving flat notice that he would never again speak to me upon any subject whatever.

Wade made a brave effort to stand by his resolve. To my very contrite apology in the morning he turned a deaf ear. Getting himself a hasty breakfast, he kicked into his ski and pushed off down the Mammoth Springs road at four o'clock. When Carr and I started an hour later a drizzling rain had set in, making the going the hardest and most disagreeable of the whole trip. The snow, honey-combed by the rain, offered no support to our ski, and we wallowed to our knees in soft slush. The drizzle increased to a steady downpour as the morning advanced, drenching our clothes till the water ran down and filled our rubber shoes. Buckskin gauntlets soaked through faster then they could be wrung out. It was not long before chilled hands became almost powerless to grasp the slippery steering poles and numbing fingers fumbled helplessly in their efforts to tighten the stretching thongs of rawhide that bound on our ski.

Wade was spitting a steady stream of curses where we pulled up on his heels at the mud flats by Beaver Lake, but sullenly refused to make way for me to take the lead and break trail. Past Obsidian Cliff, on the still half-frozen pavement of broken glass, the going was better, and I managed to pass and cut in ahead of the wallowing watchman just before we came to the long avenue of pines running past Crystal Springs. He seemed barely able to drag one sagging knee up past the other, and his half-averted face was seamed deep with lines of weariness. Only the spasmodic movement of his lips told of the unborn curses that his overworked lungs lacked the power to force forth upon the air.

Realizing from the fact that he lacked the breath to curse how desperately near a collapse the fellow must be, I whipped up my own flagging energies with the idea of pushing on ahead to the cabin and getting a fire started and a pot of coffee boiling. Shouting to Carr to stand by to bring in the remains, I spurted on as fast as I could over the crust which was still far from rotted by the rain. I was a good three hundred yards ahead of my companions when I turned from the road to cross Obsidian Creek to the cabin. A glance back before I entered the trees revealed Wade reeling drunkenly from side to side, with Carr hovering near to catch him when he fell.

A large fir log spanned the deep half-frozen pool beyond which stood the half-snow-buried cabin. The near bank was several feet higher than the far, so that the log sloped downward at a sharp angle. Since, on our outward trip, we had crossed successfully by coasting down the snow-covered top of the log, I assumed that the feat might be performed again, especially as I was far more adept of the ski now than then. But I failed to reckon on the softening the snow had undergone in the elapsed fortnight. Half-way over the whole right side of the slushy cap sliced off and let me flounder down into the waist-deep pool.

Wade, so Carr says, seemed to sense instantly the meaning of the wild yell that surged up from the creek, and the realization of the glad fact that his tormentor had come a cropper at the log acted like a

33

galvanic shock to revive his all-but-spent energies. I had just got my head above the slushy ice and started cutting loose my ski thongs when he appeared on the bank above. There was triumph in his fatigue-drawn visage, but no mirth. Such was the intensity of his eagerness to speak that for a few moments the gush of words jammed in his throat and throttled coherence. Then out it came, short, sharp and to the point.

"Now, gol dern ye—what d'ye think o' God now?" was all he said. Then he kicked out of one of his ski and reached it down for me to climb out by. We did not, nor shall, resume the argument. The man is too terribly in earnest. He has the same spirit—with the reverse English on it, of course—that I had taken for granted had died with the early martyrs.

Mammoth Hot Springs, April 25.

The outside world of ordinary people has pushed in and taken possession of Fort Yellowstone in the fortnight since I left here, and the invasion of the rest of the Park will speedily follow. Two hundred labourers for road work and the first installment of the hotel help arrived last night and today they are swarming over the formations, gaping into the depths of the springs, and setting nails and horseshoes to coat and crust in the mineral-charged water as it trickles down the terraces. Irish and Swedes predominate among both waitresses and shovel-wielders, and as they flock about, open-mouthed with wonder and chattering at the tops of their voices, they remind one of a throng of immigrants just off the steamer. More of the same kind are due today, and still more tomorrow. Then, worst of all, in another week will come the tourists. But Lob, the good god of the snows and all his works will be gone by then, thank heaven, and so shall I. Today there has come a letter from "Yankee Jim" stating that he has located a boat which he reckons will do for a start down the Yellowstone. He fails to say what he reckons it will do after it starts, but I shall doubtless know more on that score at the end of a couple of days.

Bannock hunting party by Frederic Remington 1895

IV - RUNNING "YANKEE JIM'S CANYON"

Thirty or forty years ago, before the railway came, "Yankee Jim" held the gate to Yellowstone Park very much as Horatius held the bridge across the Tiber. Or perhaps it was more as St. Peter holds the gate to heaven. Horatius stopped all-comers, while Jim, like St. Peter, passed all whom he deemed worthy—that is to say, those able to pay the toll. For the old chap had graded a road over the rocky cliffs hemming in what has since been called "Yankee Jim's Canyon of the Yellowstone," and this would-be Park tourists were permitted to travel at so much per head. As there was no other road into the Park in the early days, Jim established more or less intimate contact with all visitors, both going and coming. As there were several spare rooms in his comfortable cabin home at the head of the Canyon, many, like Kipling, stopped over for a few days to enjoy the fishing. The fishing never disappointed them, and neither did Jim.

But people found Jim interesting and likable for very diverse reasons—that became plain to me before ever I met the delicious old character and was able to form an opinion of my own. A city official of Spokane who had fished at Jim's canyon sometime in the nineties characterized him to me as the most luridly picturesque liar in the Northwest. A few days later a fairly well known revivalist, who shared my seat on the train to Butte, averred that "Yankee Jim" was one of the gentlest and most saintly characters he ever expected to meet outside of heaven. This same divergence of opinion I found to run through all the accounts of those who had written of Jim in connection with their Park visits. He had undoubtedly poured some amazingly bloodthirsty stories into the ready ears of the youthful Kipling when the latter, homeward bound from India, visited the Yellowstone in the late eighties. Some hint of these yarns is given in the second volume of "From Sea to Sea." Yet it could not have been much earlier than this that Bob Ingersoll and Jim struck sparks, when the famous orator endeavoured to expound his atheistic doctrines on the lecture platform in Livingston. And the witty Bob admitted that on this occasion he found himself more preached against than preaching.

It remained for the Sheriff of Park County, whom I met in Livingston on my way to the Park, to reveal the secret spring of Jim's dual personality. "It all depends upon whether old 'Yankee' is drinking or not," he said. "He puts in on an average of about five days lapping up corn juice and telling the whoppingest lies ever incubated on the Yellowstone and ten days neutralizing the effects of them by talking and living religion. Latterly he's been more and more inclining to spiritualism and clairvoyance. Tells you what is going to happen to you. Rather uncanny, some of the stuff he gets off; but on the whole a young fellow like you that's looking for copy will find him to pan out better when the black bottle's setting on the table and the talk runs to Injun atrocities. But you're sure to get spirits in any event—if old 'Yankee' isn't pouring 'em he'll be talking with 'em."

"Spirits are good in any form," I said, nodding gravely and crooking a finger at the bar-keeper of the old Albermarle; "but—yes—without doubt the black bottle promises better returns from my standpoint."

But it was not to be, either sooner or later. Silver of beard and of hair and lamb-gentle of eye, old 'Yankee' fairly swam in an aura of benevolence when I dropped in upon him a couple of days later—and the table was bare. He raised his hands in holy horror when I asked him to tell me Injun fighting stories, and especially of the tortures he had seen and had inflicted. He admitted that such stories had been attributed to him, but couldn't imagine how they had got started. He had lived with the Crows and the Bannocks, it was true, but only as a friend and a man of peace, never as a warrior. Far from ever having been even a passive spectator of torture, he had always exerted himself to prevent, or at least to minimise it. And he flattered himself that his efforts along this line had not been without success. He felt that no village in which he had lived but had experienced the civilizing effect of his presence.

Of course all this was terribly disappointing to a youth who had read of the hair-raising exploits of "Yankee Jim, the White Chief," in yellow-backed shockers, and who had looked forward for weeks to hearing from his thin, hard lips the story of the burning of the squaw at the stake, immortalized by Kipling. Forewarned, however, that it was something like ten to five against my stumbling upon the felicitude of a black-bottle régime, I philosophically decided to go ahead with my ski trip through the Park on the chance that the process of the seasons might bring me better luck on my return. After inducing Jim to undertake either to find or to build me a boat suitable for my contemplated down-river trip, I pushed on to Fort Yellowstone.

Whether the sign of the black bottle wheeled into the ascendant according to calendar reckoning during the three weeks of my absence I never learned. Certainly there was no sign of it either above or below the horizon on my return. Jim was more benevolent than ever, and also (so he assured me almost at once) in direct communication with his "little friends up thar." He tried hard to dissuade me from tackling the river, urging that a fine upstanding young feller like myself ought to spend his life doing good to others rather than going outer his way to do harm to hisself. I chaffed him into relinquishing that line by asking him if he was afraid I was going to bump the edges off some of his canyon scenery. Finally he consented to take me up-river to where an abandoned boat he had discovered was located, but only on condition I should try to get another man to help me run the Canyon. He said he would give what help he could from the bank, but didn't care to expose his old bones to the chance of a wetting. He thought "Buckskin Jim" Cutler, who owned a ranch nearby, might be willing to go with me as far as Livingston. He was not sure that Cutler had run the Canyon, but in any event he knew it foot by foot, and would be of great help in letting the boat down with ropes at the bad places.

We found the craft we sought about a mile up-stream, where it had been abandoned at the edge of an eddy at the last high-water. It was high and dry on the rocks, and the now rapidly rising river had some ten or twelve feet to go before reaching the careened hull. Plain as it was that neither boat-builder nor even carpenter had had a hand in its construction, there was still no possible doubt of its tremendous strength and capacity to withstand punishment. Jim was under the impression that the timbers and planking from a wrecked bridge had been drawn upon in building it. That boat reminded me of the pictures in my school history of the Merrimac, and later, on my first visit to the Nile, the massive Temple of Karnak reminded me of that boat.

Jim said that a homesick miner at Aldridge had built this fearful and wonderful craft with the idea of using it to return to his family in Hickman, Kentucky. He had bade defiance to the rapids of the Yellowstone with the slogan "HICKMAN OR BUST." The letters were still discernible in tarry bas relief. So also the name on bow and stern. (Or was it stern and bow? I was never quite sure which was which.) Kentucky Mule he had called it, but I never knew why till years later. And sorry I was I ever learned, too.

The fellow was lacking in heart, Jim said. He had run no rapids to speak of in the Mule, and if she had hit any rocks in the five or six miles of comparatively open water above she had doubtless nosed them out of the way. The principal trouble appeared to have been that she preferred to progress on her side or on her back rather than right side up. This had caused her to fill with water, and that, while apparently not affecting her buoyancy greatly, had made her cabin uncomfortable. Her owner abandoned her just as soon as she could be brought to bank, selling what was salvable of his outfit and leaving the rest. What Jim complained of was the chap's failure to live up to his slogan. Nothing had busted except his nerve. He hoped that in case I did push off I wouldn't disgrace myself—and him, who was sponsoring me, so to speak—by not keeping going. Old Jim had good sound basic instincts. No doubt about that.

Working with ax and crowbar, we finally succeeded in knocking off the cabin of what had been intended for a houseboat, leaving behind a half-undecked scow. It was about twenty-five feet in length, with a beam of perhaps eight feet. The inside of this hull was revealed as braced and double-braced with railroad ties, while at frequent intervals along the water lines similar timbers had been spiked, evidently for the purpose of absorbing the impact of rocks and cliffs. She was plainly unsinkable whatever side was upward, but as it was my idea to ballast her in an endeavour to maintain an even keel, I went over her caulking of tarry rags in the hope of reducing leakage to a minimum. We also hewed out and rigged a clumsy stern-sweep for steering purposes, and it was my intention to have a lighter one at the bow in the event I was able to ship a crew to man it. I didn't care a lot for looks at this juncture as I was going to rebuild the Mule at Livingston in any case.

With the aid of a couple of chaps from a neighbouring ranch, we launched her down a runaway of cottonwood logs into the rising backcurrent of the eddy. It was not yet sunset, so there was still time to stow a heavy ballasting of nigger-head boulders before dark. Water came in for a while, but gradually stopped as the dry pine swelled with the long-denied moisture. She still rode high after receiving all of a thousand pounds of rocks, but as I did not want to reduce her freeboard too much

I let it go at that. She was amazingly steady withal, so that I could stand on either rail without heaving her down more than an inch or two. She looked fit to ram the Rock of Gibraltar, let alone the comparatively fragile banks and braes of "Yankee Jim's Canyon." Never again has it been my lot to ship in so staunch a craft.

Returning at dusk to Jim's cabin, we had word that "Buckskin Jim" Cutler was away from home and not expected back for several days. That ended my search for a crew, as there appeared to be no other eligible candidates. Of "Buckskin Jim" I was not to hear for twenty years, when it chanced that he was again recommended to me as the best available river-man on the upper Yellowstone. How that grizzled old pioneer fought his last battle with the Yellowstone on the eve of my push-off from Livingston for New Orleans I shall tell in proper sequence.

Jim insisted on casting my "horryscoop" that night, just to give me an idea how things were going to shape for the next week or two. Going into a dark room that opened off the kitchen, he muttered away for some minutes in establishing communication with his "little friends up thar." Finally he called me in, closed the door, took my hand and talked balderdash for a quarter of an hour or more. I made note in my diary of only three of the several dozen things he told me. One was: "Young man, you have the sweetest mother in all the world"; another: "I see you struggling in the water beside a great black boat"; and the third: "You will meet a dark woman, with a scowling face, to whom you will become much attached."

Now that "sweetest mother" stuff was ancient stock formula of the fortune-telling faker, and considering what Jim knew of my immediate plans it hardly seemed that he needed to get in touch with his "little friends up thar" to know that there was more than an even break that I was going to be doing some floundering around a big black boat; but how in the deuce did the old rascal know that I was going to meet the one and only "Calamity Jane" the following week in Livingston?

Jim was bubbling with reminiscence when he came out of his averred trance, but only in a gentle and benevolent vein. He claimed that he was able to prove that Curley, the Crow Scout, was not a real survivor of the Custer massacre, but only witnessed a part of the battle from concealment in a nearby coulée. When I pressed him for details, however, he seemed to become suspicious, and switched off to a rather mild version of his meeting with Bob Ingersoll.

"Bob and his family stopped a whole day with me," he said, "and we got to be great friends. His girls came right out here into this kitchen where you are sitting now and helped me wash the dishes. They was calling me 'Uncle Jim' before they had been here an hour. Well, the people down there persuaded Bob to give a lecture in Livingston, and I drove down the whole forty miles to hear it. When the lecture was over Bob came up to me in the Albermarle and asked me what I thought of it. 'Mr. Ingersoll,' said I, 'I don't like to tell you.' 'I like a man that speaks his mind,' says he; 'go on.' 'Well, Mr. Ingersoll,' said I, 'I think you're making a grievous mistake in standing there and hurting the feelings, and shaking the faith, of almost the whole audience, just for the sake of the one or two as thinks as you do.' At first I thought he was going to come back at me, but all of a sudden he laughed right out in his jolly way, and took my arm and said, 'Mr. George, let's have a drink.' Bob, in spite of his pernishus doctrines, was the most lovable man I ever met."

Now this was a very different account of the clash from the one I had heard in Livingston. There I was assured that the debate took place at the Albemarle bar about midnight, and that Jim had Bob's hide on the fence at the end of five minutes of verbal pyrotechnics. But it was characteristic of Jim that he would neither boast nor talk of Injuns during his non-drinking periods. Doubtless, therefore, he was far from doing himself justice in relating the Ingersoll episode. I surely would like to have heard it when the sign of the black bottle was in the ascendant.

Jim admitted a clear remembrance of Kipling's visit, but was chary of speaking of it, doubtless on account of the squaw-at-the-stake story. (His atrocity yarns troubled him more than any other when they came home to roost, so they assured me in Livingston.) Of Roscoe Conkling his impressions were not friendly, even in the benevolence of his present mood. "Conkling caught the biggest fish a tourist ever caught in the Canyon," he said, "He was a great hand with a rod, but, in my candid opinion, greatly over-rated as a public man. He had the nerve to cheat me out of the price of a case of beer. Ordered it for a couple of coachloads of his friends and then drove off without paying for it. Yes, possibly a mistake; but these politicians are slippery cusses at the best."

Our plan of operation for the morrow was something like this: Bill and Herb, the neighbouring ranchers, were to go up and help me push off, while Jim went down to the first fall at the head of the Canyon to be on hand to pilot me through. If I made the first riffle all right, I was to try to hold up the boat in an eddy until Jim could amble down to the second fall and stand-by to signal me my course into that one in turn. And so on down through. Once out of the Canyon there were no bad rapids above Livingston. I was to take nothing with me save my camera. My bags were to remain in Jim's cabin until he had seen me pass from sight below the Canyon. Then he was to return, flag the down train from Cinnabar, and send the stuff on to me at Livingston. Looking back on it from the vantage of a number of years' experience with rough water, that decision to leave the luggage to come on by train was the only intelligent feature of the whole plan.

Steering a boat in swift water with any kind of a stern oar is an operation demanding a skill only to be acquired by long practice. For a greenhorn to try to throw over the head of a craft like Kentucky Mule was about comparable to swinging an elephant by the tail. This fact, which it took me about half a minute of pulling and tugging to learn, did not bother me a whit however. I felt sure the Mule was equal to meeting the Canyon walls strength for strength. I knew I had considerable endurance as a swimmer, and I was fairly confident that a head that had survived several seasons of old style mass-play football ought not to be seriously damaged by the rocks of the Yellowstone. Well, I was not right—only lucky. Not one of the considerations on which my confidence was based really weighed the weight of a straw in my favour. That I came out at the lower end comparatively unscathed was luck, pure luck. Subsequently I paid dearly for my initial success in running rapids like a bull at a gate. In the long run over-confidence in running rough water is about as much of an asset as a millstone tied round the neck. Humility is the proper thing; humility and a deep distrust of the wild beast into whose jaws you are poking your head.

As I swung round the bend above the head of the Canyon I espied old Jim awaiting my coming on a rocky coign of vantage above the fall. A girl in a gingham gown had dismounted from a calico pony and was climbing up to join us. With fore-blown hair and skirt she cut an entrancing silhouette against the sun-shot morning sky. I think the presence of that girl had a deal to do with the impending disaster, for I would never have thought of showing off if none but Jim had been there. But something told me that the exquisite creature could not but admire the sang froid of a youth who would let his boat drift while he stood up and took a picture of the thundering cataract over which it was about to plunge. And so I did it—just that. Then, waving my camera above my head to attract Jim's attention to the act, I tossed it ashore. That was about the only sensible thing I did in my run through the Canyon.

As I resumed my steering oar I saw that Jim was gesticulating wildly in an apparent endeavour to attract my attention to a comparatively rock-free chute down the left bank. Possibly if I had not wasted valuable time displaying my sang froid I might have worried the Mule over in that direction, and headed right for a clean run through. As it was, the contrary brute simply took the bit in her teeth and went waltzing straight for the reef of barely submerged rock at the head of the steeply cascading pitch of white water. Broadside on she sunk into the hollow of a refluent wave, struck crashingly fore and aft, and hung trembling while the full force of the current of the Yellowstone surged against her up-stream gunwale.

Impressions of what followed are considerably confused in my mind, but it seems to me things happened in something like the following order: The pressure on her upper side heeled the Mule far over, so that her boulder ballast began to shift and spill out at the same time the refluent wave from below began pouring across the down-stream gunwale. The more she heeled the more ballast she lost and the more water she shipped. Fortunately most of the boulders had gone before the pin of the stern-sweep broke and precipitated me after the ballast. The few niggerheads that did come streaming in my wake were smooth and round and did not seem to be falling very fast when they bumped my head and shoulders. Certainly I hardly felt them at the time, nor was I much marked from them afterwards.

Sticking to my oar I came up quickly and went bobbing down the undulating stream of the rapid, kissing off a rock now and then but never with sharp impact. I had gone perhaps a hundred yards when the lightened boat broke loose above and started to follow me. Right down the middle of the riffle she came, wallowing mightily but shipping very little additional water. Holding my oar under one arm and paddling lightly against the current with my other, I waited till the Mule floundered abreast of me and clambered aboard. She was about a third full of water, but as the weight of it hardly compensated for the rocks dumped overboard she was riding considerably higher than before, though much less steadily.

Looking back up-stream as the reeling Mule swung in the current, I saw Jim, with the Gingham Girl in his wake, ambling down the bank at a broken-kneed trot in an apparent endeavour to head me to the next fall as per schedule. Poor old chap! He was never a hundred-to-one shot in that race now that the Mule had regained her head and was running away down mid-channel regardless of obstacles. He stumbled and went down even as I watched him with the tail of my eye. The Gingham Girl pulled him to his feet and he seemed to be leaning heavily against her fine shoulder as the Mule whisked me out of sight around the next bend. That was the last I ever saw of either of them. Jim, I understand, died some years ago, and the Gingham Girl.... Dear me, she must be forty herself by now and the mother of not less than eight. Even ten is considered a conservative family up that way. They are not race suicidists on the upper Yellowstone.

With the steering oar permanently unshipped there was more difficulty than ever in exercising any control over the balkiness of the stubborn Mule. After a few ineffectual attempts I gave up trying to do anything with the oar and confined my navigation to fending off with a cottonwood pike-pole. This really helped no more than the oar, so it was rather by good luck than anything else that the Mule hit the next pitch head-on and galloped down it with considerable smartness. When she reeled through another rapid beam-on without shipping more than a bucket or two of green water I concluded she was quite able to take care of herself, and so sat down to enjoy the scenery. I was still lounging at ease when we came to a sharp right-angling notch of a bend where the full force of the current was exerted to push a sheer wall of red-brown cliff out of the way. Not unnaturally, the Mule tried to do the same thing. That was where I discovered I had over-rated her strength of construction.

I have said that she impressed me at first sight as being quite capable of nosing the Rock of Gibraltar out of her way. This optimistic estimate was not borne out. That little patch of cliff was not high enough to make a respectable footstool for the guardian of the Mediterranean, but it must have been quite as firmly socketed in the earth. So far as I could see it budged never the breadth of a hair when the Mule, driving at all of fifteen miles an hour, crashed into it with the shattering force of a battering-ram. Indeed, everything considered, it speaks a lot for her construction that she simply telescoped instead of resolving into cosmic star-dust. Even the telescoping was not quite complete. Although there were a number of loose planks and timbers floating in her wake, the hashed mass of wood that backed soddenly away from the cliff and off into the middle of the current again had still a certain seeming of a boat—that is, to one who knew what it was intended for in the first place. With every plank started or missing, however, water had entered at a score of places, so that all the buoyancy she retained was that of floating wood.

The Mule had ceased to be a boat and become a raft, but not a raft constructed on scientific principles. The one most desirable characteristic of a properly built raft of logs is its stability. It is almost impossible to upset. The remains of the Mule had about as much stability as a toe-dancer, and all of the capriciousness. She kept more or less right side up on to the head of the next riffle and then laid down and negotiated the undulating waves by rolling.

It was not until some years later, if I remember aright, that stout women adopted the expedient of rolling to reduce weight. The Mule was evidently well in advance of the times, for she reduced both weight and bulk by all of a quarter in that one series of rolls. I myself, after she had spilled me out at the head of the riffle, rode through on one of her planks, but it was a railroad tie, with a big spike in it, that rasped me over the ear in the whirlpool at the foot.

And so I went on through to the foot of "Yankee Jim's Canyon." In the smoother water I clung to a tie, plank or the thinning remnants of the Mule herself. At the riffles, to avoid another clout on the head from the spike-fanged flotsam, I found it best to swim ahead and flounder through on my own. I was not in serious trouble at any time, for much the worst of the rapids had been those at the head of the Canyon. Had I been really hard put for it, there were a dozen places at which I could have crawled out. As that would have made overtaking the Mule again somewhat problematical, I was reluctant to do it. Also, no doubt, I was influenced by the fear that Jim and the Gingham Girl might call me a quitter.

Beaching what I must still call the Mule on a bar where the river fanned out in the open valley at the foot of the Canyon, I dragged her around into an eddy and finally moored her mangled remains to a friendly cottonwood on the left bank. Taking stock of damages, I found that my own scratches and bruises, like Beauty, were hardly more than skin deep, while the Mule, especially if her remaining spikes could be tightened up a bit, had still considerable rafting potentialities. As the day was bright and warm and the water not especially cold, I decided to make way while the sun shone—to push on as far toward Livingston as time and tide and my dissolving craft would permit. But first for repairs.

Crossing a flat covered with a thick growth of willow and cotton-wood, I clambered up the railway embankment toward a point where I heard the clank of iron and the voices of men at work. The momentary focus of the section gang's effort turned out to be round a bend from the point where I broke through to the right-of-way, but almost at my feet, lying across the sleepers, was a heavy strip of rusty iron, pierced at even intervals with round holes. Telling myself that I might well go farther and fare worse in my quest for a tool to drive spikes with, I snatched it up and returned to the river. Scarcely had my lusty blows upon the Mule's sagging ribs begun to resound, however, than a great commotion broke forth above, which presently resolved itself into min-gled cursings and lamentations in strange foreign tongues. Then a howling-mad Irish section-boss came crashing through the underbrush, called me a train-wrecker, grabbed the piece of iron out of my hand, and, shouting that he would "sittle" with me in a jiffy, rushed back to the embankment.

The fellow seemed to attach considerable importance to that strip of rusty iron. Why this was I discovered a couple of minutes later when I found him and three Italians madly bolting it to the loose ends of a couple of rails before the down-bound train hove in sight up the line.

"I'll larn ye to steal a fish-plate, ye snakin' spalpheen," he roared as the train thundered by and disappeared around the bend.

"I didn't steal any fish-plate," I remonstrated quaveringly, backing off down the track as the irate navvy advanced upon me brandishing a three-foot steel wrench; "I only borrowed a piece of rusty iron. I didn't see any fish-plate. I didn't even know where your lunch buckets are. I wish I did, for I've just swum through the Canyon and I'm darned hungry." Gad, but I was glad the Gingham Gown and "Yankee Jim" couldn't see me then!

With characteristic Hibernian suddenness, the bellow of rage changed to a guffaw of laughter. "Sure an' the broth o' a bhoy thot a fish-plate wuz a contryvance fer to eat off uv! An' it's jest through the Canyon he's swam! An' it's hoongry an' wet thot he is! Bejabbers then, we won't be afther murtherin' him outright; we'll jest let him go back to the river an' dhrown hisself! Stip lively, ye skulkin' dagoes, an' bring out the loonch."

And so while I sat on the bank quaffing Dago Red and munching garlic-stuffed sausages, Moike and his gang of Eyetalians abandoned their four-mile stretch of the Northern Pacific to drive more spikes in the Mule's bulging sides and render her as raft-shape as possible for a further run. The boss led his gang in a cheer as they pushed me off into the current, and the last I saw of him he was still guffawing mightily over his little fish-plate joke. As a matter of fact, since Mike in his excitement appeared to have neglected to send out a flagman when he discovered his fish-plate was missing, I have always had a feeling that the northbound train that morning came nearer than I did to being wrecked in "Yankee Jim's Canyon of the Yellowstone."

The rest of that day's run was more a matter of chills than thrills, especially after the evening shadows began to lengthen and the northerly wind to strengthen. The Mule repeated her roll-and-reduce tactics every time she came to a stretch of white water. There were only three planks left when I abandoned her at dusk, something over twenty miles from the foot of the Canyon, and each of these was sprinkled as thickly with spike-points as a Hindu fakir's bed of nails. One plank, by a curious coincidence, was the strake that had originally borne the defiant slogan. "HICKMAN OR BUST." Prying it loose from its cumbering mates, I shoved it gently out into the current. There was no question that Kentucky Mule was busted, but it struck me as the sporting thing to do to give that plank a fighting chance to nose its way down to Hickman. If I had known what I learned last summer I should not have taken the trouble. Hickman has had more "Kentucky Mule" than is good for it all the time; also a huge box factory where soft pine planks are cut up into shooks. The last of my raft deserved a better fate. I hope it stranded on the way.

Spending the night with a hospitable rancher, I walked into Livingston in the morning. There I found my bags and camera, which good old "Yankee Jim" had punctually forwarded by the train I had so nearly wrecked. The accompanying pictures of Jim and his Canyon are from the roll of negatives in the kodak at the time.

Calamity Jane c. 1880

V - "CALAMITY JANE"

Thrilled with the delights of swift-water boating as they had been vouchsafed to me in running the Mule through "Yankee Jim's Canyon," I hastened to make arrangements to continue my voyage immediately upon arriving in Livingston. A carpenter called Sydney Lamartine agreed to build me a skiff and have it ready at the end of three days. Hour by hour I watched my argosy grow, and then—on the night before it was ready to launch—came "Calamity."

In every man's life there is one event that transcends all others in the bigness with which it bulks in his memory. This is not necessarily the biggest thing that has really happened to him. Usually, indeed, it is not. It is simply the thing that impresses most deeply the person he happens to be at the time. The thunderbolt of a living, breathing "Calamity Jane" striking at my feet from a clear sky is my biggest thing. One does his little curtsey to a lot of queens, real and figurative, in the course of twenty years' wandering, but not the most regal of them has stirred my pulse like the "Queen of the Plains." Queens of Dance, Queens of Song, and Queens of real kingdoms, cannibalistic and otherwise, there have been, but only one "Queen of the Rockies." And this was not because "Calamity Jane" was either young, or beautiful or good. (There may have been a time when she was young, and possibly even good, but beautiful—never.) So far as my own heart-storm was concerned, it was because she had been the heroine of that saffron-hued thriller called "The Beautiful White Devil of the Yellowstone," the which I had devoured in the hay-mow in my adolescence. The fragrance of dried alfalfa brings the vision of "Calamity Jane" before my eyes even to this day. She is the only flesh-and-blood heroine to come into my life.

My initial meeting with "Calamity" was characteristic. It was a bit after midnight. On my way home to the old Albemarle to bed I became aware of what I thought was a spurred and chap-ed cowboy in the act of embracing a lamp-post. A gruff voice hailed me as I came barging by. "Short Pants!" it called; "oh, Short Pants—can't you tell a lady where she lives?"

"Show me where the lady is and I'll try," I replied, edging cautiously in toward the circle of golden glow.

"She's me, Short Pants—Martha Cannary—Martha Burk, better known as 'Calamity Jane.'"

"Ah!" I breathed, and again "Ah!" Then: "Sure, I'll tell you where you live; only you'll have to tell me first." And thus was ushered in the greatest moment of my life.

"Calamity," it appeared, had arrived from Bozeman that afternoon, taken a room over a saloon, gone out for a convivial evening and forgotten where she lived. She was only sure that the bar-keeper of the saloon was named Patsy, and that there was an outside stairway up to the second story. It was a long and devious search, not so much because there was any great number of saloons with outside stairways and mixologists called Patsy, as because every man in every saloon to which we went to inquire greeted "Calamity" as a long-lost mother and insisted on shouting the house. Then, to the last man, they attached themselves to the search-party. When we did locate the proper place, it was only to find that "Calamity" had lost her room-key. After a not-too-well-ordered consultation, we passed her unprotesting anatomy in through a window by means of a fire-ladder and reckoned our mission finished. That was the proudest night on which I am able to look back.

When, agog with delicious excitement, I went to ask after Mrs. Burk's health the following morning. I found her smoking a cigar and cooking breakfast. She insisted on my sharing both, but I compromised on the ham and eggs. She had no recollection whatever of our meeting of the previous evening, yet greeted me as "Short Pants" as readily as ever. This name, later contracted to "Pants," was suggested by my omnipresent checkered knickers, the only nether garment I possessed at the time.

The "once-and-never-again 'Calamity Jane,'" was about fifty-five years of age at this time, and looked it, or did not look it, according to where one looked. Her deeply-lined, scowling, sun-tanned face and the mouth with its missing teeth might have belonged to a hag of seventy. The rest of her-well, seeing those leather-clad legs swing by on the other side of a signboard that obscured the wrinkled phiz, one might well have thought they belonged to a thirty-year-old cow-puncher just coming into town for his night to howl. And younger even than her legs was "Calamity's" heart. Apropos of which I recall confiding to Patsy, the bar-keep, that she had the heart of a young god Pan. "Maybe so," grunted Patsy doubtfully (not having had a classical education he couldn't be quite sure, of course); "in any case she's got the voice of an old tin pan." Which was neither gallant nor quite fair to "Calamity." Her voice was a bit cracked, but not so badly as Patsy had tried to make out. Another thing: that black scowl between her brows belied the dear old girl. There was really nothing saturnine about her. Hers was the sunniest of souls, and the most generous. She was poor all her life from giving away things, and I have heard that her last illness was contracted in nursing some poor sot she found in a gutter.

Naturally, of course, after a decent interval, I blurted out to "Calamity" that I had come to hear the story of her wonderful life. Right gamely did the old girl come through. "Sure, Pants," she replied. "Just run down and rush a can of suds, and I'll rattle off the whole layout for you. I'll meet you down there in the sunshine by those empty beer barrels."

It was May, the month of the brewing of the fragrant dark-brown Bock. Returning with a gallon tin pail awash to the gunnels, I found "Calamity" enthroned on an up-ended barrel, with her feet comfortably braced against the side of one of its prostrate brothers. Depositing the nectar on a third barrel at her side, I sank to my ease upon a soft patch of lush spring grass and budding dandelions. "Calamity" blew a mouthhole in the foam, quaffed deeply of the Bock; wiped her lips with a sleeve, and began without further preliminary:

"My maiden name was Martha Cannary. Was born in Princeton, Missouri, May first, 1848." Then, in a sort of parenthesis: "This must be about my birthday, Pants. Drink to the health of the Queen of May, kid." I stopped chewing dandelion, lifted the suds-crowned bucket toward her, muttered "Many happy Maytimes, Queen," and drank deep. Immediately she resumed with "My maiden name was Martha Cannary, etc."... "As a child I always had a fondness for adventure and especial fondness for horses, which I began to ride at an early age and continued to do so until I became an expert rider, being able to ride the most vicious and stubborn horses.

"In 1865 we emigrated from our home in Missouri by the overland route to Virginia City, Montana. While on the way the greater part of my time was spent in hunting along with the men; in fact I was at all times with the men when there was excitement and adventure to be had. We had many exciting times fording streams, for many of the streams on the way were noted for quicksand and boggy places. On occasions of that kind the men would usually select the best way to cross the streams, myself on more than one occasion having mounted my pony and swam across the stream several times merely to amuse myself and had many narrow escapes; but as pioneers of those days had plenty of courage we overcame all obstacles and reached Virginia City in safety.

"Mother died at Blackfoot in 1866, where we buried her. My father died in Utah in 1867, after which I went to Fort Bridger. Remained around Fort Bridger during 1868, then went to Piedmont, Wyoming, with U. P. railway. Joined General Custer as a scout at Fort Russell, Wyoming, in 1870. Up to this time I had always worn the costume of my sex. When I joined Custer I donned the uniform of a soldier. It was a bit awkward at first but I soon got to be perfectly at home in men's clothes.

"I was a scout in the Nez Percé outbreak in 1872. In that war Generals Custer, Miles, Terry and Cook were all engaged. It was in this campaign I was christened 'Calamity Jane.' It was on Goose Creek, Wyoming, where the town of Sheridan is now located. Captain Egan was in command of the post. We were ordered out to quell an uprising of Indians, and were out several days, had numerous skirmishes during which six of the soldiers were killed and several severely wounded. On returning to the post we were ambushed about a mile from our destination. When fired upon Captain Egan was shot. I was riding in advance and on hearing the firing turned in my saddle and saw the Captain reeling in his saddle as though about to fall. I turned my horse and galloped back with all haste to his side and got there in time to catch him as he was falling. I lifted him onto my horse in front of me and succeeded in getting him safely to the fort. Captain Egan on recovering laughingly said: 'I name you "Calamity Jane," the Heroine of the Plains.' I have borne that name up to the present time."

Here, little dreaming what the consequence would be, I interrupted, and for this reason: I had felt that "Calamity" had been doing herself scant justice all along, but in the "christening" incident her matter-of-fact recital was so much at variance with the facts as set down in "The Beautiful White Devil of the Yellowstone" that I had to protest. "Excuse me, Mrs. Burk," I said, "but wasn't that officer's name Major Percy Darkleigh instead of Egan? And didn't you cry 'For life and love!' when you caught his reeling form? And didn't you shake your trusty repeater and shout 'To hell with the redskins!' as you turned and headed for the fort? And didn't you ride with your reins in your teeth, the Major under your left arm and your six-shooter in your right hand? And when you had laid the Major safely down inside the Fort, didn't he breathe softly, 'I thank thee Jane from the bottom of a grateful heart. No arm but thine shall ever encircle my waist, for while I honour my wife—'"

Here "Calamity" cut in, swearing hard and pointedly, so hard and pointedly, in fact, that her remarks may not be quoted verbatim here. The gist of them was that "The Beautiful White Devil of the Yellowstone" was highly coloured, was a pack of blankety-blank lies, in fact, and of no value whatever as history. I realize now that she was right, of course, but that didn't soften the blow at the time.

Trying to resume her story, "Calamity," after groping about falteringly for the thread, had to back up again and start with "My maiden name was Martha Cannary." She was in a Black Hills campaign against the Sioux in 1875, and in the spring of '76 was ordered north with General Crook to join Generals Miles, Terry and Custer at the Big Horn. A ninety-mile ride with dispatches after swimming the Platte brought on a severe illness, and she was sent back in General Crook's ambulance to Fort Fetterman. This probably saved her from being present at the massacre of the Little Big Horn with Custer and the 7th Cavalry.

"During the rest of the summer of '76 I was a pony express rider, carrying the U. S. mails between Deadwood and Custer, fifty miles over some of the roughest trails in the Black Hills. As many of the riders before me had been held up and robbed of their packages, it was considered the most dangerous route in the Hills. As my reputation as a rider and quick shot were well known I was molested very little, for the toll-gatherers looked on me as being a good fellow and they knew I never missed my mark.

"My friend William Hickock, better known as 'Wild Bill,' who was probably the best revolver shot that ever lived, was in Deadwood that summer. On the second of August, while setting at a gambling table of the Bella Union Saloon, he was shot in the back of the head by the notorious Jack McCall, a desperado. I was in Deadwood at the time and on hearing of the killing made my way at once to the scene of the shooting and found that my best friend had been killed by McCall. I at once started to look for the assassin and found him at Shurdy's butcher shop and grabbed a meat cleaver and made him throw up his hands, through excitement on hearing Bill's death having left my weapons on the post of my bed. He was then taken to a log cabin and locked up, but he got away and was afterwards caught at Fagan's ranch on Horse Creek. He was taken to Yankton, tried and hung."

Here, forgetting myself, I interrupted again in an endeavour to reconcile the facts of "Wild Bill's" death as just detailed with the version of that tragic event as depicted in "Jane of the Plain." "Calamity's" language was again unfit to print. "Wild Bill" had not expired with his head on her shoulder, muttering brokenly "My heart was yours from the first, oh my love!" Nor had she snipped off a lock of Bill's yellow hair and sworn to bathe it in the heart-blood of his slayer. All blankety-blank lies, just like the "White Devil." Then, as before, in order to get going properly, she had to back up and start all over with: "My maiden name was Martha Cannary." This time I kept chewing dandelions and let her run on to the finish, thereby learning the secret of her somewhat remarkable style of delivery. This is the way the story of her life concluded:

"We arrived in Deadwood on October 9th, 1895. My return after an absence of so many years to the scene of my most noted exploits, created quite an excitement among my many friends of the past, to such an extent that a vast number of citizens who had heard so much of 'Calamity Jane' and her many adventures were anxious to see me. Among the many whom I met were several gentlemen from eastern cities, who advised me to allow myself to be placed before the public in such a manner as to give the people of the eastern cities the opportunity of seeing the lady scout who was made so famous during her daring career in the West and Black Hills countries. An agent of Kohl and Middleton, the celebrated museum men, came to Deadwood through the solicitation of these gentlemen, and arrangements were made to place me before the public in this manner. My first engagement to begin at the Palace Museum, Minneapolis, January 20th, 1896, under this management.

Hoping that this history of my life may interest all readers, I remain, as in the older days,

"Yours,

"Mrs. M. Burk,

"Better known as 'Calamity Jane.'"

"Calamity" had been delivering to me her museum tour lecture, the which had also been printed in a little pink-covered leaflet to sell at the door. That was why, like a big locomotive on a slippery track, she had had to back up to get going again every time she was stopped. Oh, well, the golden dust from the butterfly wing of Romance has to be brushed off sometime; only it was rather hard luck to have it get such a devastating side-swipe all at once. That afternoon for the first time I began to discern that there was a more or less opaque webbing underlying the rainbow-bright iridescence of sparkling dust.

With "Calamity Jane," the heroine, evanishing like the blown foam of her loved Bock, there still remained Martha Burk, the human document, the living page of thirty years of the most vivid epoch of Northwestern history. Compared to what I had hoped from my historic researches in the pages of "The Beautiful White Devil of the Yellowstone," this was of comparatively academic though none the less real interest. Reclining among the dandelions the while "Calamity" oiled the hinges of her memory with beer, I conned through and between the lines of that record for perhaps a week. Patiently diverting her from her lecture platform delivery, I gradually drew from the strange old character much of intimate and colourful interest. Circulating for three decades through the upper Missouri and Yellowstone valleys and gravitating like steel to the magnet wherever action was liveliest and trouble the thickest, she had known at close range all of the most famous frontier characters of her day. Naturally, therefore, her unrestrained talk was of Indians and Indian fighters, road-agents, desperadoes, gamblers and bad men generally—from "Wild Bill" Hickock and "Buffalo Bill" Cody to Miles and Terry and Custer, to "Crazy Horse," "Rain-in-the-Face," Gall and "Sitting Bull." She told me a good deal of all of them, not a little, indeed, which seemed to throw doubt on a number of popularly accepted versions of various more or less historical events. I made notes of all of her stories on the spot, and at some future time of comparative leisure, when there is a chance to cross-check sufficiently with fully established facts from other sources, I should like to make some record of them. These pages are not, of course, the place for controversial matter of that kind.

One morning I kept tryst among the dandelions in vain. Inquiry at the saloon revealed the fact that "Calamity," dressed in her buckskins, had called for her stabled horse at daybreak and ridden off in the direction of Big Timber. She would not pay for her room until she turned up again, Patsy said. It was a perfectly good account, though; she never failed to settle up in the end. I never heard of her again until the papers, a year or two later, had word of her death.

With Romance and Historical Research out of the way, my mind returned to the matter of my river voyage. Giving the newly built skiff a belated trial with Sydney Lamartine, we swamped in a comparatively insignificant rapid and shared a good rolling and wetting. Agreed that the craft needed higher sides, we dragged it back to the yards for alterations. Sydney thought he might find time to complete them inside of a week. Before that week was over I had one foot in a newspaper editorial sanctum and the other on the initial sack of a semi-professional baseball team. As both footings seemed certain to develop into stepping-stones to the realization of the most cherished of my childhood's ambitions (I had never cared much about being President), the river voyage to the Gulf went into complete discard—or rather into a twenty-year postponement.

I became an editor as a direct consequence of making good on the ball team; I ceased to be an editor as a direct consequence of betraying a sacred trust laid upon me by the ball team. This was something of the way of it: Livingston had high hopes of copping the championship of the Montana bush league, which, at the time of my arrival, was just budding into life with the willows and cottonwood along the river. For this laudable purpose a fearful and wonderful aggregation had been chivvied together from the ends of baseballdom, numbering on its roster about as many names that had once been famous in diamond history as those that were destined to become so. Of the team as finally selected three or four of us were known to the police, and at least two of us came into town on brake-beams. One of us was trying to forget the dope habit, and another—our catcher and greatest star—had just been graduated from a rum-cure institute.

All of us were guaranteed jobs—sinecural in character of course. Paddy Ryan, one of the pitchers, and two or three others were bar-keepers. There was also one night-watchman, one electrician and one compositor. I was rather a problem to the management until the editor of the Enterprise was sent to the same institute recently evacuated by our bibulous catcher. Then I was put in his place—I mean that of the editor. I don't seem to recall much of my editorial duties or achievements, save that one important reform I endeavoured to institute—that of getting a roll of pink paper and publishing the Enterprise as a straight sporting sheet—somehow fell through.

They tried me out at centre in the opening game against Billings, and after the second—at Bozeban—I became a permanency at first-base, my old corner at Stanford. Besides holding down the initial bag, I was told off for the unofficial duty of guarding the only partially rum-cured catcher—seeing that he was kept from even inhaling the fumes of the seductive red-eye, a single séance with which meant his inevitable downfall for the season.

I played fairly promising ball right along through that season, and but for the final disaster which overtook me in my unofficial capacity as Riley's keeper might have gone on to the fulfillment of my life ambition. Up to the final and deciding series with Butte I kept my thirsty ward under an unrelaxing rein, with the result that he played the greatest baseball of his career. Then a gang of Copper City sports, who had been betting heavily on the series, contrived to lure Riley away for a quarter of an hour while I was taking a bath. He was in the clouds by the time I located him, and rapidly going out of control into a spinning nose-dive. He crashed soon after, and when I left him just as the dawn was breaking through the red smoke above the copper smelters he was as busy chasing mauve mice and purple cockroaches as the substitute we put in his place that afternoon was with passed balls. To cap the climax—in endeavouring to extend a bunt into a two-bagger, or some equally futile stunt—I strained an old "Charley Horse" and went out of the game in the second inning. We lost the game, series and championship, and I, incidentally, ceased to be a rising semi-pro ball player and a somewhat less rising country editor.

I have failed to mention that I did have one more fling at the Yellowstone that summer. Lamartine remodelled his skiff as we had planned, and one Sunday when Livingston had a game on at Big Timber we decided to make the run down by river. Pushing off at daybreak we arrived under the big bluff of Big Timber a good hour or two before noon. I find this run thus celebrated in an ancient clipping from the Livingston Post, contemporary of the Enterprise.

"Mr. L. R. Freeman, Mr. Armstrong and Sydney Lamartine made the trip from this city to Big Timber last Sunday in a flat-bottomed boat. The river course between this city and Big Timber is fully 50 miles, and the gentlemen made the trip without mishap in six hours. Several times the boat had narrow escapes from being turned over, but each time the skill of the boatmen prevented any trouble. Quite a crowd assembled on the Springdale bridge and watched the crew shoot the little craft through the boiling riffle at that point, cheering them lustily for the skill they displayed in swinging their boat into the most advantageous places. The trip is a hazardous one, but full of keen enjoyment and spice and zest. The time made is without doubt the fastest river boating ever done on the Yellowstone, and it is extremely doubtful if the record has been duplicated on any other stream. Mr. Freeman, who has had considerable experience in boating in Alaska, says that he never has seen a small boat make such splendid time."

I don't remember a lot about that undeniably speedy run save that we stopped for nothing but dumping water out of the boat. Last summer, with a number of seasons of swift-water experience to help, I took rather more than nine hours to cover the same stretch. I suppose it was because the river and I were twenty years older. Age is a great slower down, at least where a man is concerned. I do seem to recall now that I stopped a number of times on this last run to see which was the smoother channel. Doubtless the old Yellowstone was just as fast as ever.

Calamity Jane in her kitchen in Livingston, Montana

PART II: DOWN THE YELLOWSTONE

I - PRESENT-DAY YELLOWSTONE PARK

In embarking anew on a journey from the Continental Divide to the mouth of the Mississippi I was influenced by three considerations in deciding to start on the Yellowstone rather than on one of the three forks of the Missouri. There was the sentimental desire to see again the land of geysers and hot springs and waterfalls, no near rival of which had I ever discovered in twenty years of travel in the out-of-the-way places of the earth. Then I wanted to go all the way by the main river, and there was no question in my mind that the Yellowstone was really the main Missouri, just as the Missouri was the main Mississippi. John Neihardt has put this so well in his inimitable "River and I" that I cannot do better than quote what he has written in this connection.

"The geographer tells us that the mouth of the Missouri is about seventeen miles above St. Louis, and that the mouth of the Yellowstone is near Buford, North Dakota. It appeared to me that the fact is inverted. The Missouri's mouth is near Buford, and the Yellowstone empties directly into the Mississippi. I find that I am not alone in this opinion. Father de Smet and other early travellers felt the truth of it; and Captain Marsh, who has piloted river craft through every navigable foot of the entire system of rivers, having sailed the Missouri within sound of the Falls and the Yellowstone above Pompey's Pillar, feels that the Yellowstone is the main stem and the Missouri a tributary.

"Where the two rivers join, even at low water, the Yellowstone pours a vast turbulent flood, compared with which the clear and quieter Missouri appears an overgrown rain-water creek. The Mississippi after some miles obliterates all traces of its great western tributary; but the Missouri at Buford is entirely lost in the Yellowstone within a few hundred yards. All of the unique characteristics by which the Missouri River is known are given it by the Yellowstone—its turbulence, its tawniness, its feline treachery, its giant caprices."

I cannot agree with Mr. Neihardt that the Mississippi obliterates the Missouri within a few hundred yards, or even a few hundred miles; for in all but name it is the latter, not the former, that mingles its mud with the Gulf of Mexico. But in his contention that the Yellowstone is the dominant stream where it joins the Missouri he is borne out by all that I saw and the opinion of every authority I talked with, from a half-breed river-rat at Buford to the Army engineers at Kansas City.

My third reason for choosing the Yellowstone was the technical consideration of superior "boatability." The head of continuous small-boat navigation on the Yellowstone is about at the northern boundary of the Park, at an elevation of over five thousand feet. On the Missouri it is at Fort Benton, below the cataracts of Great Falls, whose elevation is less than half that of Gardiner. As the distance from these respective points to the junction of the two rivers near the Montana-North Dakota line is about the same, it is evident that the rate of fall of the Yellowstone is many times greater than that of the Upper Missouri below Benton. Indeed, the figures are, roughly, 3000 feet fall for the former and 500 for the latter. This means that the Yellowstone is much the swifter stream and, being also of considerably greater volume, is infinitely preferable to the boatman who does not mind more or less continuous white water. In addition to these points, the fact that the Yellowstone, from the Park to its mouth, flows through one of the most beautiful valleys in America while the Missouri meanders a considerable distance among the Bad Lands, makes the former route the pleasanter as well as the swifter one. These considerations, pretty well in my mind before I started, were more than borne out in every respect by my subsequent experience. There are two or three large rivers down which boats (by frequent linings and portagings) can be taken which are of greater fall than the Yellowstone, but I know of none anywhere in the world on which such fast time can be made as on the latter—this because its rapids are all runnable.

As I was not out for records of any description upon this trip, it was no part of my plan to start from the remotest source of the Yellowstone, some twenty-five miles south of the southern boundary of the Park, but rather simply to follow down from the most convenient point where the Continental Divide tilted to that river's upper water-shed. Following the river as closely as might be by foot through the Park, it was then my purpose to take train to Livingston and resume my voyage from about where it had been abandoned two decades previously. As the steel skiff I had ordered was extremely light, and of a type quite new to me, I did not care to make my trial run through "Yankee Jim's Canyon."

I entered the Park on June 21st, the second day of the season, by the West Yellowstone entrance. This route, following up the valley of the Madison, was hardly more than opened up on the occasion of my former visit. At that time the nearest railway point was Monida, on the Oregon Short Line. Now I found the Union Pacific terminus chock-ablock with the boundary at West Yellowstone, and fully as many tourists coming in by this entrance as by the northern gateway at Gardiner. The eastern entrance, by Cody, was also regularly served by the transportation company, while a southerly road to the Snake was open for auto traffic. The accessibility of the Park had been increased many-fold.

Probably more than ninety-five per cent. of the tourists visiting the Yellowstone are fluttered folk and wild being rushed through on a four-day schedule. This imposes a terribly hectic program, which, however, is not the fault of the transportation or hotel people, (who offer all facilities and inducements for a calmer survey), but of the tourist himself, who seems imbued with the idea that the more he sees in the day the more he is getting for his money. The American tourist, doubtless a quite mild-demeanoured and amenable person on his native heath, when observed flagrante delicto touring is by long odds the worst-mannered of all of God's creatures. Collectively, that is; individually many of him and her turn out far from offensive. Strangely—perhaps because, for the moment, they are all more or less infected with the same form of hysteria—they never seem to get much on each other's nerves. To a wanderer, however, habituated to the kindness, consideration, dignity and respect for age commonly displayed by such peoples as the Red Indian, the South Sea Islander and the Borneo Dyak, the tourist at close range is rather trying. I proceeded with the regular convoy to Old Faithful, then took a car to the crest of the Continental Divide, and proceeded from there down the Yellowstone on foot in comparative peace and contentment.

With the large and rapidly increasing number of railway tourists coming to the Park every year, each intent upon making the round and getting away in the minimum of time, there is probably no better plan devisable than the present one of shooting them in and out, and from camp to camp, in large busses. The most annoying and unsatisfactory feature of this system is the great amount of time which the tourist must stand by waiting for his bus-seat and room to be allotted. This, however, can hardly be helped with daily shipments numbering several hundred being made from and received at each camp and hotel. Under the circumstances the most satisfactory way of touring the Park is in one's own car, stopping at either hotel or camp, according to one's taste and pocketbook. Delightful as the auto camping grounds are, tenting is hardly to be recommended on account of the mosquitoes.

Allowing for the difference in season, there was little change observable in the natural features of the Park since my former visit. Things looked different, of course, but that was only because there was less snow and more dust. The only appreciable natural changes were in the hot spring and geyser areas, where here or there a formation had augmented or crumbled to dust according to whether or not its supply of mineral-charged water had been maintained or not. The cliffs and mountains, waterfalls, and gorges could have suffered no more than the two decades, infinitesimal geologic modifications—mostly erosive. Even in the geyser basins the changes of a decade are such as few save a scientific observer would note. The first authentic written description of the Fire Hole geysers basins was penned nearly eighty years ago by Warren Angus Ferris, a clerk of the American Fur Company. It describes that region of the present as accurately as would the account of a last summer's tourist.

Not unless we are prepared to accept those delectable yarns of old Jim Bridger as the higher truth is there any evidence that the natural features of the Park have suffered material change since its discovery. But even in his own credulous time people were hardly inclined to swallow the story of that cliff of telescopic glass which tempted Jim into shooting twenty-five-miles-distant elk under the impression that it was grazing within gunshot. Nor would those ancient sceptics believe the story of the way the hoofs of Bridger's horse were shrunk to pinpoints in crossing the Alum Creek, or of how those astringent waters actually shrunk the land and reduced the distance he had to travel. Indeed, it is hard to believe these stories even today. And yet Bridger is credited with being the greatest natural topographer in frontier history—he was said to be able to draw an accurate map of the Rocky Mountains on a buffalo hide.

But if the natural changes in the Yellowstone appeared inappreciable, the artificial, the evolutionary changes were very striking. Roads and trails had been greatly improved and extended, horse-drawn vehicles had given place to motors, and the Rangers of the National Park Service had taken over policing and patrol from the Army. Most heartening of all, Administration seemed at last to have found itself. In the decade or two following the creation of the Park, there were two Superintendents, Langford and Norris, who gave the best that was in them to an all but thankless task. Greatly hampered by lack of co-operation and even by actual obstruction in Washington the achievement of neither was commensurate with his effort.

Besides Langford and Norris these earlier years saw two or three political appointees at the head of Park affairs, men whom no less an authority than Captain Chittenden intimates were either incompetent or corrupt. It was largely the lamentable results of the administration or these latter that was responsible for turning the Yellowstone over to the Army, just as was done in the construction of the Panama Canal. The Army, subject to the limitations of military administration for this kind of work, came through as usual with great credit to itself. A military Superintendent—Capt. George W. Goode—was in charge on the occasion of my first visit, and at that time it seemed probable that the army régime might be continued indefinitely. It was plain, however, that an officer who might be sent from the Philippines to the Yellowstone one year, and from the Yellowstone to Alaska the next, was not in a position, no matter what his ability and enthusiasm, to do full justice to the task in hand. What appeared to be needed was a civil administration, with the right sort of men, backed up with sympathy and vigour at Washington. That is the desideratum which seems to have been arrived at, both as to men and the support at the National Capital.

If I were going to pay adequate tribute to what the National Park Service is doing and trying to do I should want the rest of this volume in which to express myself. So I shall only say in passing that, judging from the members of that service I have met, including the Superintendent and Assistant Superintendent of the Yellowstone, it seems to me to be developing a type that does not suffer in comparison with that fine idealist, the British Civil Servant, whom I have always admired so unreservedly where I have found him at work in India, the Federated Malay States, and other outposts of empire—an official of ability and experience giving his lifetime for the good of others for very modest pay. If I knew how to pay a higher compliment I should do so. In concluding this chapter I shall touch briefly on the future plans and policy of the National Park Service for the Yellowstone.

It was a comparatively modest affluent of Yellowstone Lake that I followed down from the two-ways-draining marsh on the Continental Divide. I did not come upon the Yellowstone proper until I reached the outlet of the Lake. It is a splendid stream even there—broad, deep, swift and crystal-clear. At a point very near where the bridge of the Cody road crosses the river is the site of the projected Yellowstone Lake Dam, a dangerous encroachment of power and irrigation interests which the energetic efforts of the National Park Service appear now to have disposed of for good.

From my previous recollection of the river from the outlet to the Upper Falls I had the impression that perhaps the first six or eight miles of this stretch, with careful lining at one or two rapids, might be run with an ordinary skiff. Finding a number of small fishing boats moored just below the outlet I endeavoured to hire one with the idea of settling this point in my mind. The boatman refused to entertain my proposition for a moment, not even when I offered to deposit the value of the skiff in question. "I don't care if you reckon you can swim out of one of them rapids," he said with finality. "My boat can't swim, and a boat earns its value three times over in a good season." He was a practical chap, that one. Why, indeed, shouldn't it worry him more to have his boat go over the Falls than it would to have me do it?

Walking down from the Lake to the Canyon I used the road only where it ran close to the river. Thus I not only came to a more intimate acquaintance with the latter, but also avoided the blended dust and gasoline wakes of the daily Hegira of yellow busses. At the first rapid—an abrupt fall of from three to six feet formed by a ledge of bedrock extending all the way across the river—I found countless millions of trout bunched where that obstacle blocked their upward movement to the Lake. I had seen salmon jumping falls on many occasions, but never before trout. These seemed to be getting in each other's way a good deal, but even so were clearing the barrier like a flight of so many grasshoppers. Many that got their take-off correctly gauged made a clean jump of it. Others, striking near the top of the fall, still had enough kick left in their tails to drive on up through the coiling bottle-green water.

But most of those that struck below the middle of the fall were carried back and had their leap for nothing.

Immediately under the fall the fish were so thick that thrusting one's hand into a pool near the bank was like reaching into the bumper haul of a freshly-drawn seine. Closing a fist on the slippery creatures was quite another matter, however. I was all of twenty minutes throwing half a dozen two and three-pounders out onto the bank. Stringing these on a piece of willow, I carried them up to the road and offered them as a present to the first load of campers that came along. They appeared to be from Kansas, or Missouri or thereabouts, and so had quite a discussion before accepting them—didn't seem quite agreed as to whether the fish were fresh or not. Finally I handed one of them the string and went back to the trail by the river. They were still so engrossed in their debate that it never occurred to them to say "Thank you." Ford owners are nearly always suspicious I have found, and notably so when they come from Pike County or environs.

There is a magnificent stretch of rapids for a quarter of a mile or more above the Upper Falls, where the river takes a running start for its two major leaps. I spent all of an hour lounging along here, speculating as to just how far a man might get in with a boat—and then get out. On a quiet, sunny day, with the mind at peace with the world, I am certain I would not venture beyond the first sharp pitch above the bridge. Fleeing from Indians, tourists or a jazz orchestra, however, I am inclined to think I would chance it for all of three hundred yards. Possibly even, in the event it were either of the two latter that menaced, I would chance the Falls themselves.

To me the Grand Canyon of the Yellowstone is more inspiring—in a perfectly human, friendly sort of way—than any other of the great sights of the world. There are others that are on a bigger scale and more awesome—the Grand Canyon of the Colorado or the snows of Kinchinjunga from Darjeeling, for examples,—but to the ordinary soul these are too stupendous for him to grasp, they appeal rather than thrill. There may be a few exalted, self-communing souls, like Woodrow Wilson and William Randolph Hearst, who could look the Grand Canyon of the Colorado right between the eyes and feel quite on a par with it—nay, even a bit condescending perhaps. Lesser mortals never quite get over catching their breath at the more than earthly wonder of it. I have never seen any one save a present-day flapper gaze for the first time on the sombre depths of the great gorge of the Colorado with untroubled eyes.

The Grand Canyon of the Yellowstone is not like that—it exhilarates like a glass of old wine, a fresh sea breeze, a master-piece of painting. There are no darksome depths to awaken doubt. You can see right to the bottom of the gorge from almost any vantage point you choose. But it is the rainbow-gaiety of the brilliant colour streaking that gives the real kick. That gets over with all and sundry—and grows on them. The ones to whom the Canyon appeals most are those who have seen it most frequently.

Twenty years ago I attempted, in the diary of my winter ski tour, some description of the snow-choked gorge of the Yellowstone as I glimpsed it from the rim. One learns a vast quantity of various kinds of things in two decades, among them a realization of the numerous occasions on which he has been an ass. I shall try not to offend again by attempting to describe Grand Canyons.

I descended to the river at several points in the Canyon, but found it quite impossible to proceed down stream any distance in the bottom of the gorge. The fall is tremendous all the way through and I doubt if there are many stretches of over a few hundred yards in length in which a boat could live. The total fall from the Lake to the foot of the Grand Canyon is something like three thousand feet, probably not far from a hundred feet to the mile. I cannot recall offhand a river of so great a volume anywhere in the world that has so considerable a fall. The Indus, in the great bend above Leh, in Ladakh, may approximate such a drop, and so may the Brahmaputra, where it cleaves the main range of the Himalayas after passing Lhassa. The Yangtse, where it comes tumbling down from the Tibetan plateau into Szechuan, is hardly more than a mountain torrent. With the possible exception of the main affluents of the Upper Amazon in the Peruvian Cordillera, these are the only great rivers in the running for a record of this kind.

In walking from the Grand Canyon to Mammoth Hot Springs I followed the road over Mount Washburn, stopping for the night at Camp Roosevelt, below Tower Falls. This most recently established of the Park camps takes its name from the fact that it is located on the spot where Roosevelt and John Burroughs made headquarters on the occasion of their winter tour of the Yellowstone a decade and a half ago.

The best fishing in the Park is found in this section, and for that reason the management has developed and maintained it very largely as a sporting camp. Only those with a really genuine love of the out-of-doors stop there, while the regular ruck of the tourists pass it by. Those facts alone set it apart in a class by itself as the pleasantest spot in the Park for a prolonged sojourn.

On account of the class of people it attracts, Roosevelt has been made rather a pet of the management from its inception. This is especially true of personnel. The wholly charming couple—a Kentucky gentleman and his wife—whom I found in charge last summer presided over the camp as over a country home in the Blue Grass. The staff—all college boys and girls—was practically a complete Glee Club in itself. Good sports, too. Roosevelt was the only camp at which I did not find myself consumed with longing for the primeval solitude of the Park as I had known it on my winter tour—during the closed season for tourists.

Mammoth Hot Springs, in spite of the passing of Fort Yellowstone, I found to have augmented greatly since my former visit. Most of my old friends were gone, however, Assistant Superintendent Lindsay being the only one remaining who recalled my coming and going. In company with a couple of officers from the Post we had, I believe, enjoyed an afternoon of fearful and wonderful tennis on the still ice- and snow-covered court. Federal Judge Meldrum, terror of poachers, had been in the party twenty years ago, but said he did not remember me. I was rather glad he had had no occasion to. Had I ever been connected with the geyser that Private Ikey Einstein soaped, or with aiding and abetting Sergeant Hope to drive a flock of sheep over the bluffs into the Gardiner River, the Judge would doubtless have been able to refer to the official memoranda to jog his memory—possibly some thumb prints and a side and front view of my criminal phiz.

To my great regret I learned that F. Jay Haynes, official photographer of the Park, had died but a few months before. In his place I found Jack Haynes, his son, who is brilliantly maintaining the reputation of his illustrious father, both as an artist and as a factor in forwarding the destiny of the Yellowstone. What the intrepid Kolb Brothers are doing in photographing the Grand Canyon of the Colorado, what Byron Harmon is doing in the Canadian Rockies, that the Haynes family have done for the Yellowstone Park. I say "have done," because their work, having been carried on during nearly four decades, is much more nearly complete than that of the others who have worked a shorter time in a rather less concentrated sphere.

But F. Jay Haynes was far more than a great photographic artist. He was a great lover of the out-of-doors generally and of that of Yellowstone Park particularly. In his organization of the transportation companies to serve respectively the east and west entrances to the Park, it was the bringing of the latter to the people that was the main consideration in his mind; the financial success of his ventures was secondary. I believe these were successful on both counts, however. I know that Mr. Haynes is given the credit for inducing the late E. H. Harriman to build a branch of the Union Pacific to the western entrance of the Park, now the principal portal so far as number of tourists is concerned. They have recently done the memory of Mr. Haynes the honour of naming a mountain after him. This is a fitting tribute, and well deserved. Far more impressive a monument, however, are his pictures. Mount Haynes may be seen for a distance of perhaps a hundred miles; the Yellowstone photographs of F. Jay Haynes may be seen at the ends of the world.

Jack Haynes is trying to do everything his father did, both as an artist and as a friend of the Yellowstone. He was on the ground early. He claims to have had his first ride over the Park roads some thirty years ago—in a baby carriage. Now he burns up those same roads in a Stutz roadster, taking hours to make the Grand Circuit where his father took days or weeks. A Ranger at the Canyon told me that Jack made the round so fast that he often headed back into Norris before the dust from his outward trip had settled down. I think that is somewhat exaggerated; yet Judge Meldrum, who trundled Jack on his knee, has figured that the latter's time for some of his rounds averages about twice the speed limit. The old judge swears that it is his dearest ambition to soak the boy good and plenty for his defiance of Uncle Sam's laws—when he catches him at it. So far, however, the only times that the Judge has had any really unimpeachable evidence in point was when he himself was a passenger in Jack's car! Then, he confesses, he couldn't take out his watch because he was using both hands to hold on. Nor would the watch have been of any use anyhow, he further admits, for they were going so fast that the mile-posts looked just like a white stone wall, with a very impressionistic black streak along near the top where the numbers came!

Not so far behind Jim Bridger and his telescopic glass cliff, that little touch about the mile-posts. And it proves that John Colter's dash from his Indian captors can't always hope to stand as a speed record. Surely it is good to know that the best of ancient Yellowstone tradition is being so well maintained.

Jack Haynes drove me down to meet Superintendent Horace M. Albright, who had only returned to Mammoth a couple of hours before I had to leave to catch my train at Gardiner. I had Mr. Albright very much in mind when I tried to pay the most fitting compliment I could to the type of men that are being drawn to the National Park Service. An ever-ready sneer from the common run of political heelers for the man in office who is trying to accomplish something for the common good in a decent and honourable manner is "impractical idealist." The words are all but inseparably linked from long usage. Indeed, it seems rarely to occur to anybody that there might be such a thing as a practical idealist. And yet just that is what Horace M. Albright impressed me as being; and such, I would gather from all I can learn, is his Chief, Stephen T. Mather, Director of the National Park Service. No one will question that they are idealists, I daresay. That they are also practical, I doubt not that very strong affirmative admissions might be secured from a number of baffled politicians who have tried to encroach upon Yellowstone Park with power and irrigation schemes.

Captain Chittenden, writing of the early days of the Yellowstone, speaks of the menace of the railways—attempts on the part of certain companies to build into or through the Park itself. That threat was disposed of in good time. The railways accepted the "Thus far shalt thou go and no farther!" as final, built as close as practicable to the boundaries, and rested content with allowing transportation within the Park to be carried on by horse-drawn vehicles, later to be replaced by motor busses. The menace of the railways was no longer heard of, but in time a new one arose—that of the power and irrigation interests. This hydra-headed camel tried to crawl under the flap of the Park tent in the form of a dam at the outlet of Yellowstone Lake for the ostensible purpose of preventing floods on the lower river. The bill to authorize the project was introduced in Congress by Senator Thomas P. Walsh and bears his name. Two very practical idealists, called to step into the breach almost at a moment's notice, were able to demolish every claim made for the measure after scarcely more than a hurried reading of it. These two were Superintendent Albright and George E. Goodwin, Chief Engineer of the National Park Service. Mr. Albright, practically offhand, showed the falsity or the fallacy of every contention made in the bill as regards the Park itself, but perhaps the solar plexus was delivered by Mr. Goodwin, when he introduced figures to show that all of the floods on the lower river came a month previous to high water in Yellowstone Lake—that they were directly due in fact, not to the latter, but to the torrential spring discharges of the Big Horn, Tongue, Powder and other tributaries of the main stream.

This blocked the measure at the time, and equally telling action from the Department of Interior has checked every subsequent attempt to advance it. I should really like to know the particular practical idealist of that Department who dissected a circular letter sent out under Mr. Walsh's signature to his Congressional colleagues. Perhaps it was Stephen T. Mather himself, head of the National Park Service. At any rate, the blows dealt were so sharp and jolting that reading the statement somehow made me think of a man walking down a row of plaster images and cracking them with a hammer. If I was not certain this insincere and maladroitly handled bill would not be at rather more than its last gasp before these pages appear in print I would write more about it—that is, against it. As things have shaped, however, this will hardly be necessary.

In explaining why it was that the National Park Service had rallied its forces for so vigorous a defence of the citadel against the Walsh Bill, Mr. Albright quoted the words of John Barton Payne, Secretary of the Interior under Wilson, in pushing the Jones-Esch Bill, which returned the national parks and monuments to the sole authority of Congress. Said Mr. Payne: "When once you establish a principle that you can encroach on a national park for irrigation or water power, you commence a process which will end only in the commercialization of them all.... There is a heap more in this world," he concluded, "than three meals a day."

I was sorry not to be able to see more of Horace M. Albright. One can put up with a good deal of his kind of practical idealism.

Shoshone Falls, as it appeared c. 1871

II - LIVINGSTON TWENTY YEARS AFTER

The train on which I journeyed from the Park to Livingston was a bit late in getting started for some reason, as a consequence of which it was trying to make up the lost time all the way. It was a decidedly rough passage, especially on the curves through the rocky walls of "Yankee Jim's Canyon." Even so, however, I reflected that the careening observation car was making a lot better weather of it than did the old Kentucky Mule twenty years before.

Although past the crest of its spring rise by nearly a fortnight, the Yellowstone was considerably higher than the early May stage at which I ran it before. Even glimpsed from the train the Canyon impressed me as having a lot of very rough water—much too rough for a small open boat to run right through. With frequent landing and careful lining, however, it looked quite feasible; indeed, on arrival at Livingston I learned that a couple of men had worked through with a light canoe the previous Sunday. Letting down with a line over the bad places, they took about an hour for the passage of the roughest two miles of the Canyon. My jaunt through in and about the Mule was not clocked. Although the liveliness of the action made it seem longer, I doubt if it was much over ten minutes. Nevertheless I was quite content not to have to chance it again, especially as a trial trip for a new type of boat.

Livingston is located at the bend where the Yellowstone, after running north from the Park for fifty miles, breaks from the mountains and begins its long easterly course to the Missouri through a more open valley. This was the point at which Captain Clark, temporarily separated from Lewis on their return journey from the mouth of the Columbia, first saw the upper Yellowstone. He had, of course, passed its mouth when proceeding westward by the Missouri the previous year. It was now his purpose to explore the whole length of such of the river as flowed between this point and the Missouri, making rendezvous with Lewis at some point below its mouth. Clark had come from the Three Forks of the Missouri with pack-train, but with the intention of building boats and taking to the river just as soon as trees large enough for their construction could be found. Searching every flat for suitable boat-timber, the party proceeded down the north bank of the river, probably pretty well along the route followed by General Gibbon seventy years later in the campaign against the Sioux which culminated to the Custer Massacre on the Little Big Horn.

The previous fall, rapid by rapid, I had run the lower Columbia in the wake of Lewis and Clark. Now I was turning into the trail of the Pathfinders again, this time their home trail. One of the things that I had been anticipating above all others was the delight of following that trail to its end, which also had been its beginning—St. Louis. I knew that there was going to be something of Lewis and Clark for me in every mile of the twenty-five hundred—yes, and of many another who had followed in their path. I was not to be disappointed. I only hope I am not going to be boring in telling a little about it. I trust not too much so. Darn it, a man can't be expected to write about bootleggers, and "white mule" and home-brew and ultra-modern institutions all the time. Lewis and Clark and the other pioneers of the North-west have always meant a lot to me. I simply can't help mentioning them now and again—but I'll try and strike a balance in the long run.

There was a real thrill in the tablet erected by the D. A. R. near the Livingston railway station commemorating the passing of Captain Clark. Perhaps there will be no fitter place for me to acknowledge to the Daughters of the Revolution my gratitude for many another thrill of the same kind similar monuments of theirs gave me all the way to the end of my journey. Now it was the defence of the stockade at Yankton that was celebrated, now a station of the Pony Express or a crossing of the Santa Fé Trail in Missouri, now a post on some old Indian road at Natchez. Always they were modest and fitting, and always they winged a thrill. I have never met any live Daughters of the Revolution to recognize them, but I am sure from what they have done to make the river way pleasant that they must be eminently kindly folk, like the philanthropists who erect drinking fountains for man and beast and the Burmans who put out little bird-houses in the trees.

Livingston had changed a lot since I had seen it last—that was plain before my train had swung round the long bend and pulled up at the station. The ball ground was gone—pushed right across the river by the growth of the town. Many old landmarks were missing, and the main street, lined with fine new modern buildings, had shifted a whole block west. The shade trees had grown until they arched above the clean, cool streets, now paved from one end of the town to the other.

Even the cottonwoods by the river towered higher and bulked bigger with the twenty new rings that the passing years had built out from their hearts. There was a new Post Office and a new railway station. The latter was a handsome, sizable structure, well worthy of the important junction which it served. And yet that station wasn't quite so sizable as certain of the local boosters would have people think. Here, verbatim, is what I read of it in the local Chamber of Commerce publication:

"The Northern Pacific passenger depot, which is the largest and handsomest structure of the kind on the transcontinental line between its terminals, domiciles a large number of general and division officers and covers 100 miles East, and more than that distance West on two lines and the branch railway North from this city and also the line running South." Very likely that word covers is intended to refer to the jurisdiction of the officials housed in the building, but if that sentence were to be taken literally there is no doubt that the Grand Central, Liverpool Street, the Gare du Nord and a few score more of the world's great terminals might be chucked under those hundred-mile easterly and westerly wings of the Livingston station and never be found again.

Which reminds me that Kipling also found the natives making some pretty big claims for Livingston. Something over thirty years previous to my latest visit he had stopped there over-night on his way to the Yellowstone. He describes it as a little cow-town of about two thousand. Exhausting its resources in a short stroll, he wandered off among the hills, narrowly to avoid being stepped upon by a herd of stampeding horses. He returned to the town to find it was the night before the Fourth of July, with much carousing and large talking going on. His final comment was: "They raise horses and minerals around Livingston, but they behave as though they raised cherubims with diamonds in their wings."

But this is not the Livingston of the present day, nor even the Livingston that I loved so well twenty years syne. Yes, even then almost the only ruffians and carousers were the imported ball players and editors and "Calamity Jane." The natives were very modest, gentle folk, just as they are today. And they raised several things besides horses and minerals—yea, even cherubims. I remember that distinctly, for it was one named "Bunny," who worked in the telephone office, that knitted me a purple tie which I kept for years—for a trunk-strap. It stretched and stretched and stretched, but never weakened or faded. Expressmen and other vulgar people used to think there was a bride in my party on account of that purple ribbon. Bless your heart, "Bunny!" You'll never know until you read this confession how much besides that rough, red neck of mine you snared in the loop of your purple tie.

The Livingston Enterprise had grown with the town—that was evident from a glance at the first copy to fall into my hands. Quite a metropolitan daily it was, with Associated Press service, sporting page and regular boiler-plate Fashion Hint stuff from the Rue de la Paix. The Editor, too, was a considerable advance—at least sartorially—over the one I remembered. Phillips proved a mighty engaging chap, though, and didn't seem a bit ashamed over having had me for a predecessor. People spoke of him to me as an energetic civic and temperance worker, declaring that he had been indefatigable in his efforts to put down drink all over Park County. They called his vigorous editorials on these subjects "Phillipics." They were noted for their jolt.

I modestly assured him that I couldn't claim to have done a lot for temperance during the time I sat in his chair, but that I had taken an active interest in civic reform. And then, darn him! he took down the year 1901 from the Enterprise file. I had forgotten all about that. Well, we found a number of columns of right pert comment on local men, women and events and many square feet of baseball write-ups that Phillips seemed highly tickled over; but of civic reform editorials, not a one. Or not quite so bad as that perhaps. It may be that a trenchant leader lashing the municipal council for neglecting to build a certain badly needed sidewalk would come in that class. It was a sidewalk to the baseball grounds. How well I remember the inspiration for that vitriolic attack on the City Fathers! "Bunny" lost a French-heeled slipper in the Yellowstone gumbo while mincing out to the Helena game and swore she would never appear at the Park again unless it could be done without getting muddied to her knees. "Bunny" was very outspoken for a cherubim. In those days it took an outspoken girl to mention anything between her shoe-tops and her pompadour.

I liked Editor Phillips so well that I forthwith asked him to join me for my first day's run down the river. He said he was highly complimented, but that there were a number of reasons why he would not be able to accept. The only one of these I recall was that the water was far too loosely packed between Livingston and Big Timber. Western editors are always picturesque, and Phillips was one of the best of his kind.

He mentioned two or three others who might be induced to join me for a day or two. One of these was Joe Evans, curio dealer and trapper. I am not quite sure whether it was Phillips or some one else who recommended "Buckskin Jim" Cutler as the best hand with a boat on the upper river. It took some groping in my memory to place the name, but finally I found it pigeon-holed as that of the man "Yankee Jim" had spoken of in the same connection twenty years before. I had in mind trying to get in touch with Cutler, but gave up the idea the moment I discovered Pete Holt, former Government Scout and my first guide through the Yellowstone, holding down the job of Chief of Police of Livingston. Holt's furious pace on ski had resulted in my leaving jagged fragments of cuticle on most of the trees and much of the crust along the Yellowstone Grand Tour. Here was a chance to lead a measure or two of the dance myself. Pete had ideas of his own about the looseness with which the water was packed below Livingston, but was too good a sport to let that interfere with my pleasure. Indeed, he even went out of his way to make his trip official. Two people—a man and a woman—had been drowned in the Yellowstone the previous week. He ordered himself to go in search of them in my boat, hiring Joe Evans, with his canvas canoe, to accompany us as scout and pilot. The arrangement was ideal. Joe knew the best channel—so I took it for granted,—which would leave me nothing to do but trail his wake and manage my new and untried boat. Holt's hundred and eighty pounds in the stern would give that ballast just where I needed it. The lack of serious responsibilities would give us a chance for a good old yarn while, watching my chances, I could pick favourable riffles and pay back my friend in his own coin the debt of twenty years standing.

It was a great disappointment to find no one of my old baseball team-mates still in Livingston. Jack Mjelde, Captain and second-baseman, had been killed in an electrical accident. That was a typically capricious trick of Fate. As I recall things now, Jack—a family man with a real job, and a legitimate resident of Livingston—was about the most worth preserving of the lot of us. Ed Ray had dropped in and out of town on brake-beams every now and then, and so had two or three others. Paddy Ryan, pitcher and the gentlest mannered of us all, was believed to be still a bar-keeper—somewhat surreptitiously of course. Riley, the never more than semi-Keeley-cured catcher, had last been heard of over Missoula way, and looking rather fit now that there was a more or less closed season on his favourite quarry—mauve mice.

And so it went. A score or more of old-timers who had seen me play turned up at the hotel, but only one of these brought a real thrill. That was a husky chap of about thirty, who said he had been admitted to the park once for retrieving a home-run I had swatted over the fence in a game against Anaconda. "Gosh, how you could line 'em out, boy, " volunteered some one, and grunts of assent ran back and forth through the crowd. That was all very nice, of course; but I would have enjoyed it a lot more if I could have been quite sure that none of them had been present the time we played Red Lodge on Miner's Union Day. This was the morning after the Fireman's Ball of the night before. I believe I could see the ball all right. Indeed, that was just the trouble. I saw too many balls and couldn't swing my bat against the right one. I struck out three times running. The fourth time up I connected for a mighty wallop, but only to get put out through starting for third base instead of first!

Pete Nelson, Sheriff of my former visit and now State Game Warden, called for me at the hotel and together we strolled down the old main street to the river. We had dubbed it "The-Street-That-is-Called-Straight." Just why I fail to remember, but probably some of us wanted to show his biblical learning. Riley, the Keeley-ed catcher, confessed it never had looked straight to him, and there were times—especially late on the nights we had won games—that I had doubts on that score myself. But if there had been crooks in or upon it in the old days, time had ironed them out. I especially called Nelson's attention to the Northern Pacific station at one end of the vista, the nodding cottonwoods at the other, and the glaring new concrete pavement, stretching straight as a white ribbon, connecting them up.

Pete Nelson sadly called my attention to the manner in which all the gay old palaces of carousal had been converted, and said he reckoned that perhaps every one that had patronized them had undergone the same change. I was also sad, but less optimistic than Pete respecting the increasing purpose of the ages. As we leaned on the rail of the river bridge and gazed at the swift green current I tried to recall those lines of Stevenson's which began:

"Sing me a song of a boy that is gone—
Ah, could that lad be I!"
and which conclude:
"All that was good, all that was fair,
All that was me is gone."
I couldn't remember the part that I craved, and so fell back on:
"Tears, idle tears, I know not what they mean,
Tears from the depths of some divine despair
Rise in the heart and gather to the eyes,
In looking on the happy Autumn-fields,
And thinking of the days that are no more."

That didn't quite do, either, for Tennyson was gazing on fading fields and thinking of Autumn, and I was gazing on budding cotton-woods and thinking of Spring—Spring! And yet it was a Spring that was gone.

"Pete," I said moodily, turning a gloomy eye to the seaward-rushing flood, "there's a lot of water gone under this bridge never to return, since you and I stood here last." The ex-Sheriff nodded in dreary acquiescence. "And, boy," he remarked with the weariness of the ages in his voice as he rubbed a finger up and down the bridge of a blue, cold nose that I remembered as having once glowed with all the hues of a sunset over the colour-splashed gorge of the Grand Canyon of the Yellowstone; "boy, water ain't the only thing that's gone never to return."

Arm in arm, as we had navigated "The-Street-That-is-Called-Straight" in ancient of days, we wended our way back town-ward through the gloom-drenched dusk. By devious ways and obscure Pete piloted, stopping every now and then to introduce me to certain friends as the boy who helped Livingston cop the state champeenship twenty years ago. We were treated with great deference all along the way. There was the glint of a twinkle in the ex-Sheriffian eye as Pete delivered me at the hotel. "That was just to show you, boy, that Gilead is not yet quite drained of Balm," he said, patting me on the back. "Until they give the screw a few more turns, life in little old Livingston will not be entirely without its compensayshuns."

I had dinner and spent the evening with Pete Holt's family, and a mighty wholesome interval it was after an afternoon so wild with old regrets. Holt had always been a teetotaler, and so, with nothing much to lose, faced an unclouded future. Whether, as Chief of Police, he has ever given those much-dreaded turns to the screws that would crush the last lees of pleasure from sanguine grapes of pain I have never heard. It made me think of Guelph and Ghibelline, this finding my old-time friends thus arrayed against one another. And good old Peter Nelson— I am wondering, when cock-crow sounds, if he will be found denying or denied.

"Buckskin Jim" Cutler, premier river man of the upper Yellowstone, came down to Livingston the evening before the morning I had scheduled for my departure. It had been rumoured for a couple of days that he would arrive—some said to respond to a legal summons, others that he had heard I had inquired for him and was hoping to sign on with me for my river voyage. I have never been able to make sure either way. Certainly he had been summoned to court over some dispute with a neighbour, while I have never had definite assurance that he had received any word of my trip. I could not have taken him far in any event, as I had no need of help once my boat was given a thorough trying out.

Cutler's arrival in Livingston was sudden and tragic, as is always the case when the Yellowstone takes a hand in real earnest. My boat had been set up in a blacksmith shop on the river, at the foot of the main street. Going down there just before dinner to make sure that everything was ship-shape for the start on the morrow, I found the place deserted, while there was a considerable gathering of people on the next bridge below. Starting in that direction, I met one of the helpers, breathing hard and deathly white, hurrying back to the deserted shop.

"Mighty hard luck," he ejaculated brokenly between breaths. "Man just came down past shop—in river—yelling for help. Didn't hear him till he got by. Half a minute sooner, and I could have yanked out your light boat—all set up—and picked him up. Hear they've just got him down by the next bridge—but 'fraid he's croaked. Cussed hard luck."

They were carrying a man to a waiting auto as I approached the crowd. "Yep—drowned," I heard some one say; "but he made a hell of a fight. That was old 'Buckskin Jim' to the last kick—always fighting." My glimpse of the rugged face and dripping form was of the briefest, but amply reassuring as to the truth of the statement I had overheard. It was the frame of a man that could put up a hell of a fight, and the face of a man who would—a real river-rat if there ever was one.

Next morning's issue of the Livingston Enterprise, which bore in the lower left-hand corner of its front page a modest announcement of my departure, on its upper right-hand corner carried a prominently featured account of Jim Cutler's last run on the Yellowstone. As it contains about all I have ever been able to learn in connection with the tragic finish of a character who, in 1901 as in 1921, was recommended to me as the best river hand on the upper Yellowstone, I reproduce the latter in full herewith.

Without funds to pay for transportation which would bring him into court as defendant in a water case, R. E. Cutler, Justice of the Peace at Carbella, and known throughout Park County as "Buckskin Jim," elected to travel the 40 miles to Livingston on a small raft yesterday and after riding the flood until he could leap ashore here he was pitched into the river by an overhanging limb and after struggling with the current for half a mile died either from drowning or the exertion of his fight.

Of massive physique Cutler made a wonderful fight for life despite his 65 years. A tree limb on the upper end of McLeod Island knocked the voyager from his raft. Crying for help he attempted to reach the shore, only a few feet away. Beneath the Main Street bridge, down past the tourist camp packed with tents and travellers and down river to C Street, Cutler was seen battling with the high water.

Near C Street he was forced to give up the fight. He sank but reappeared a short distance above the H Street Bridge. A. T. Toner, local contractor, swam out from the H Street Bridge and caught the floating body. Earl Kirby, mail carrier, assisted him. Miss Jane Wright, nurse at the Park Hospital, was driving by and took charge of the work of trying to restore life. Dr. P. L. Green was called and arrived in a few minutes. But all efforts were without success and death won.

Doubt as to the cause of death was voiced by officials. Some held the opinion that the deceased died from over exertion, shock or heart trouble resulting from his terrific fight against the current for a distance of more than half a mile rather than drowning.

Johnnie Doran, who was fishing near the head of McLeod Island saw Cutler knocked from the raft and hurried to give the alarm. Numerous residents along the banks of the river discovered him fighting his way down stream and numerous calls were sent to the city and county authorities. He seemed unable to make the bank but remained above water for more than four blocks.

Cutler was served with a summons to appear in Livingston tomorrow to answer to an order to show cause in a irrigation ditch dispute. When Deputy Sheriff Clarence Gilbert served the papers Mr. Cutler promised to appear but he informed the sheriff that he had no funds and would probably have to make the trip in a boat or on a raft. The officer did not take the remark seriously until Cutler was lifted from the river about 6 o'clock yesterday afternoon.

The deceased had been a prominent resident of Paradise Valley for many years. The Cutler hill on the road from Gardiner to Livingston was named after the dead man. He is survived by seven sons and one daughter besides his wife. Carbella residents reported that the deceased started down river early yesterday on a small raft intending to land at Livingston.

Hudson Bay Company trading post

III - LIVINGSTON TO BIG TIMBER

As I had planned my Yellowstone-to-New-Orleans voyage as a strictly one-man trip the ruling consideration I had had in mind in ordering my outfit was lightness and compactness. I hoped also to find serviceability in combination with these other qualifications, but the latter were the things that I insisted on in advance. Serviceability could only be proved by use. So I simply combed the sporting magazine pages, picked out the lightest, tightest boat, engine, tent, sleeping bag and other stuff I needed and let it go at that for a starter. No article that I ordered was of a type I had ever used before. If anything failed to stand up under use I knew that some sort of substitute could be provided along the way. That is one distinct advantage boating on the upper Yellowstone has over tackling such a stretch as the Big Bend of the Columbia in Canada, or the remoter waters of any of the great South American, African or Asian rivers.

First and last, of course, my boat was the main consideration. I knew that I could get on with a wooden boat as a last resort, for I had handled one alone over three hundred miles of the lower Columbia the previous season. But I wanted to give at least a try-out to something lighter than wood. I was certain there would be many occasions when my ability to take my boat completely out of the water might be the means of saving it from swamping, and possibly complete destruction. I also knew there would be many places where such things as mud or too steep a slope to the bank would make this quite out of the question with a wooden boat weighing three hundred pounds or more. Lightness, also, would mean easier pulling as well as greater mileage for the same amount of engine power.

Investigation showed that the only practicable alternatives to wood were steel and canvas. Canvas is extremely light and fairly strong, and there are occasions—such as a journey on which both overland and water travel are combined—when a properly designed folding canvas boat is incomparably preferable to any other. This is the case, however, only when there are frequent and difficult portages and very considerable distances by land to be traversed. On a comparatively unbroken river voyage the softness, the lack of rigidity, of a folding canvas boat fail by a big margin to compensate for its lightness. This consideration eliminated canvas for my purpose, though I readily grant its usefulness under conditions favourable to it.

That committed me to steel. I found various types on the market, and after several weeks of writing and wiring decided to take my chance with a fourteen-foot sectional skiff put out by the Darrow Boat Company of Albion, Michigan. The model I ordered weighed one hundred and fifty pounds, according to the catalogue, and was amply stiff and strong. I was willing to take the catalogue's word on the score of weight; the matter of strength would have to be proved. The company admitted they made no boat specially designed for rough-water work, and suggested it might be best to build me one to order with a higher side. I knew that four inches more side would be better than two, but didn't feel that I could spare the ten days the job would require. That was the reason I was taking a chance with a stock model that is probably most used for duck-hunting on lakes and marshes. My only reason for ordering a sectional type was the very considerable saving in express on account of the comparatively small amount of space required for the knocked-down boat in shipment.

I must confess that my first sight of the crated boat in the express office at Livingston was a bit of a shock. There was no question about the lightness of it, to be sure—I could pick it up, crate and all with one hand. Rather, indeed, it looked to me too light. I did not see how material so thin could withstand a collision with a sharp, mid-stream boulder without puncturing. But that was of less concern to me than the lack of freeboard. After the big batteaux and Peterboros I had used on the Columbia the previous year this bright little tin craft looked like a child's toy. Nor was there any comfort in the agent's run of patter as he stood by during my inspection. All the boat people in town had been in to see it. No end of opinions about it, but all agreed on one thing—that it wouldn't do to allow it be launched in the river. No one but a lunatic would think of such a thing, of course. Still just that kind of lunatics had been turning up every now and then; so many, indeed, that there was talk of erecting some kind of a trap down Big Timber way to catch the bodies. But I didn't look like that kind of a nut. In fact, the agent was more inclined to believe that I was one of them rich fellows from St. Paul that had a hunting lodge up in the Rockies.

I had the crate in a truck by this time. The agent's face was a study when I gave the curt order: "Blacksmith shop on river—foot of Main

Street." His was all old stuff, of course. I had heard some variation of it on every stream I had boated between the Yangtse and the Parana. Noah must have gone through a barrage of the same sort the day he laid the keel of the Ark. It didn't bother me a bit; but at the same time there was nothing cheering in it. As a matter of fact, I had still to make up my own mind as to just how much of the river those fourteen-inch sides were going to exclude in a really rough-tumbling rapid. However, it wasn't the sporting thing to do to abandon ship while ship was still in two pieces, one inside of the other, in a crate. I would wait at least until it was set up before arriving at any final verdicts. Perhaps I would even give it a trial in the water. There was a quiet eddy under the blacksmith shop, and I could play safe by bending on a line and having some one keep hold of it in a pinch.

Joe Evans, the curio dealer, rushed out, bareheaded, as I drove past his shop in the truck, to head me off from going to the river. A stranger could have no idea how treacherous the Yellowstone was, he urged. Two drownded in it already that week. If I must go ahead in that little tin pan of a boat, much better to ship it to Miles City or Glendive and put in below the worst rapids. From Livingston to Big Timber would be sheer suicide, especially for a tenderfoot in a duck-boat. Nobody knew that better than he did, for he had trapped all along the way. He was quite disinterested in warning me thus. Indeed, it was all in his favour to have me start. The county paid him twenty-five dollars a day for hunting for dead bodies in the river, with twenty-five more as bonus for every one he found. So I would see it was all to his interest to increase the spring crop of floaters; but he was a humane man, and—Thus Joe, at some length and with considerable vehemence.

I was chuckling to myself all the time Joe rattled on. The priceless old chap had been in business at the same stand twenty years ago, but it was plain he did not recognize me as the first-baseman of the Livingston champeen nine. As a matter of fact, I was just as glad that he didn't—right there before the truck-driver at least. For I had some recollection of having been with our brake-beam-riding right fielder the evening "Lefty" Clancy tried to palm a moss agate out of one of Joe's trays—and got caught. Joe made "Lefty" disgorge, and then delivered himself of remarks more pointed than polite respecting the morals of Livingston's imported ball-players.

As I have intimated, I didn't care to have that episode dragged out before the truck-driver, who might have passed it right on to Pete Holt and Editor Phillips. So I just sat tight for the moment, thanked Joe for his warnings and drove on when he got out of breath. But late that afternoon I went to his shop and made a clean breast of everything. I confessed about the moss agate, and also to the fact that I was the youth who held the steering paddle for Sydney Lamartine the time the still unbroken river record of six hours to Big Timber was put up. Then we both grinned, shook hands and apologized to each other. I apologized to Joe for seeming to have aided and abetted "Lefty" in trying to get away with the moss agate, and Joe apologized to me for that warning about the Yellowstone. There was a delicate and subtle compliment in his handsome admission that he felt that his was the greater wrong, even allowing for the fact that there were still two or three moss agates missing when he finally checked over the tray. In this latter connection, Joe said that for a year or two he had the feeling that he had made a tactical error in not turning out my pockets as well as "Lefty's" when he made his search. Then, one day, "Lefty" came in and sold him back the agates. "I didn't say anything," said Joe with a chuckle. "Just paid him a dollar apiece for the streakies, and then turned about and sold him for ten dollars an old Colt's that had laid under the snow all winter and wasn't worth six-bits. It seemed to me the kinder way," he concluded.

Of course a man of so mellow and inclusive a charity as that was easy for me to become fond of. Joe and I made friends quickly, and he fell in very readily with the plan to go along in his canvas boat when I started and help Pete Holt look for the two floaters.

Ten minutes sufficed to knock off the crate and set the boat up on the floor of the blacksmith shop. It consisted of a bow and a stern section, each about seven feet in length and provided with a thwart and a water-tight compartment. Indeed, each section was really a complete boat in itself, awkward in shape, to be sure, yet something that would float on an even keel and which could be propelled by oars or paddles. Bolting these two sections together produced a fourteen-foot skiff of astonishingly good lines. The sides, it is true, were inches lower than I would liked to have had them, but there was something distinctly heartening in the fine flare of the bows and the pronounced sheer of the little craft. Heartening, also, was the comment of the helper working to patch up a gunwale smashed in transit. He said it was the darndest hard tin he ever tried to put a drill through. Equally reassuring was the blacksmith's complaint over the trouble he was having in hammering out a number of little dents. I may as well add here that that transit-crushed gunwale was the worst scar my pretty tin toy was to show when I docked it finally in St. Louis after bumping something like 2500 miles down the Yellowstone and Missouri.

The bright little shallop looked so inherently water-worthy that I dragged it down to the river and jumped in without further misgivings. Its lightness was highly refreshing, especially when I remembered the back-breaking job it had been dragging for only a few feet the wooden skiff I had used on the lower Columbia. Built to be pulled from the forward section, carrying its load aft, it was down heavily by the head until I trimmed ship by taking in the blacksmith. My own sodden two hundred and forty pounds still brought it a bit too low by the bows, but I readily saw how the weight of my outfit and ballast would correct this until I shipped my outboard motor at Bismarck. The trial was eminently satisfactory. I dodged back and forth across the current, ran a short riffle, and then swung round and pulled right back up through it. Some water was shipped, but not enough to bother. There would be no dearth of dampness in the real rapids, I could see; but those air-chambers should float her through in one way or another, and water was easily dumped at the first eddy.

When, on pulling up to the bank to land, I tossed the painter to some one waiting below the blacksmith shop, I acknowledged the proper sex of the little craft for the first time. "Catch the line and ease her in!" was what I said, or something to that effect. That meant she had convinced me that she was a regular fellow—that I was quite game to trust myself out alone with her day or night. And that is just what I did, and for something like sixty or seventy days and nights. Saucy and spirited, and at times wilful, as she proved to be, that confidence was never betrayed.

Late that afternoon Pete Nelson called on me at the hotel, heading a delegation from the Park County Chamber of Commerce with the request that I permit the name of Livingston, Montana, to be painted upon my boat. Pete's inherent delicacy must have made him sense the fact that operating as a sandwich-man in any form was the one thing above all others from which my shrinking nature recoiled. Turning his hat nervously in his hands, the spokesman went on to explain and expatiate.

"Livingston was also the name of a great explorer. You're a sort of explorer yourself, boy. Kind of appropriate to unite the two ideas. Would also let the folks down river know that the little old town was right on the map. Full of enterprise, too, sending its emissaries on 4000-mile river voyages...."

"Back up, Pete," I cut in. "This little voyage is my own idea, not Livingston's. But go to it with the paint if you really think it will turn any settlers this way. This little old town gave me my start in life, and I am not going to lay myself open to the charge of ingratitude, no matter at what cost to my personal feelings. Only please don't insist on my flying a pennant or wearing a cap with the city slogan on it. What is the motto, by the way?"

"Live Lively in Livingston!" chanted the delegation in unison, as though delivering itself of a college yell. Pete opined it was a good slogan, with a lot of multum in parvo about it; but of course, if that was the way I felt....

The delegation bowed itself out and adjourned to a sign-painter's shop to discuss the practical side of the affair now that the diplomatic preliminaries were disposed of. The next morning I found "LIVINGSTON, MONT." streaming in bold capitals along port and starboard bows and across the stern of my argosy. The blacksmith said there had been some discussion anent blazoning the words in foot-high letters the whole length of the bottom, on the theory, it appears, that this would be the most conspicuous part of the boat in the event it capsized and continued on to New Orleans without its skipper. Whether they really carried out that inspired plan I never learned. The first sand bar I hit below Livingston would have effectually erased the letters in any event. Indeed, I was only too happy to find that it hadn't scoured a hole through the bottom itself.

We had planned to push off by nine o'clock of the morning of June thirtieth, but various odds and ends of delays and interruptions held us over an hour. Most of these were in the form of elderly ladies who had lost near relatives in the river and chose this as the fitting occasion to tell me about it. I have some recollection of speaking with a friend or connection of Sydney Lamartine. Sydney had died from some cause I made out, but whether from the river or not I did not learn. Some one else chimed in with a boat-upset story just at that juncture and things got a bit mixed. I was mighty sorry to hear about Lamartine, though. He pulled a strong oar and had no end of nerve—real river stuff.

When I came to ask the blacksmith how much I owed him, he scratched his head for a few moments and then asked if I thought a dollar would be too much. As the boat had been around his shop three or four days, with himself or a helper tinkering on little things about it much of the time out of pure kindliness, I told him I did not think it was and asked him to let me take his picture for fear I should never find another like him. I needn't have worried on that score, however. From first to last, practically all of the people I had to do with along each of the three great rivers I navigated had to be pressed before they would take any pay at all for services. Indeed, I recall but two who seriously tried to put anything over. One was the clerk of the local Ritz-Carlton at Billings, who tried to charge me two days' rent for a room I had occupied but one, and the other was a farmer's wife near Sibley, Missouri, who was going to collect twenty-five cents from me for a quart of skim milk. In the latter instance the husband of the offender came along in time to intervene in my behalf and give the woman a good tongue-lashing for trying to cheat a "po stranghah who wasn't no low down tramp no how and maybe was writin' fo the papahs." In the former case the "po stranghah" found justice denied him until he actually had to prove that he occasionally did write for the "papahs." I wouldn't have recalled either of these instances if they had chanced in the course of an ordinary trip, for the very good reason there would have been so many others of the same kind that my memory would not have compassed them all. I have remembered them, and gone to the trouble of mentioning them here, because that sort of thing isn't general practice along the river-road.

Just before starting, and purely as a gesture, I offered Pete Holt the use of my Gieve inflatable life-preserver jacket. This handy little garment I had worn in the North Sea during the war, and it had also stood me in good stead on the Columbia the previous Fall. Now I was really very keen for its reassuring embrace myself on that first day's run, and if I had thought Holt would take it I would never have offered it. When he rose to that jacket like a hungry trout to a fly I felt toward him about as one does toward a man who asks you to say "When"—and then stops pouring when you do say it. I had no legitimate complaint of course. It was entirely my own fault. Just the same, the unlucky denouement cramped my style from the outset. I had intended giving Pete a deliberate spill in some safe-looking rapid just to pay him for a few things he had done to me with the ski. I gave up the idea entirely now. That "doughnut" of air under his arms meant that he would probably bob through with dry hair while I serpentined over and under an oar. It also meant that he was going to worry a lot less about the state of the water than I hoped he would, for auld lang syne, that is. It also meant that I was going to worry rather more. It was an unfortunate move on my part altogether. Subject to that self-imposed handicap I think I did pretty well. I am sure Pete would have confessed that night that there were two or three new kinds of thrills in the world that he wotted not of before, even though that confounded "doughnut" must have acted as a good deal of a shock-absorber throughout.

Joe Evans, pushing off in his canoe from the dock of his river home a couple of hundred yards below, gave the signal for casting off. The current caught the bow as the honest blacksmith relinquished the painter and the boat swung quickly into the stream. Some boys raised a spattering cheer, the people who had lost relatives and friends in the river shook their heads dubiously, and Pete Nelson, raising three fingers aloft, shouted: "Here's luck!" He seemed a good deal elated because the Chief of Police was going away.

We were off—or nearly so. When I turned from the crowd's acclaim to con ship I discovered a good thick stream of green water slopping in, now over one quarter, now over the other. And whichever side it splashed from, Pete was getting the full benefit of it. "I hate to start crabbing at this stage, Skipper," he said with a wry grin, "but it's that confounded ballast of yours that's doing it. It's putting her rails right under."

I squinted critically down the port gunwale; then down the starboard. When she rode on an even keel either rail was a good two inches above water. But when she lurched in even the gentlest swell, one rail or the other went a good inch under. "You're right," I acquiesced. "Heave it over." One by one the units of that precious pile of junk from the blacksmith shop scrap-heap went to the bottom—a Ford axle, a mower gear, the frame of a harrow, some fragments of "caterpillar" tractor tracks, the drive wheel of a sewing machine. All of two hundred pounds of choice assorted scrap Pete heaved over, keeping but a single hunk of rusty iron that I thought I might use for an anchor at night in avoiding some pernicious stretch of mosquito coast on the lower river. She still rode low, but trimmed perfectly as soon as Pete finished bailing.

All down through the town they were waving us kindly farewells from the bank, and at the H Street bridge, where "Buckskin Jim" Cutler had been picked up the night before, we ran the gauntlet of another crowd. Then the people began to thin out and we had the river to ourselves. With the main channel streaming white a few hundred yards ahead I settled to the oars for the sharp initiatory test I knew awaited us there. We had closed up to within fifty feet of Joe by now, and saw for the first time the remarkable precautionary measures he had taken to insure the safety of himself and his canoe. For himself he had a blown-up football tied to the back of his belt, an arrangement very similar to the block of wood Chinese houseboat dwellers tie to their boy, though not to their comparatively worthless girl, children. Along both gunwales of the canoe were further air installations—these in the form of long lengths of inflated inner tubes. The practical worth of the latter contrivances was to be proved inside of half a minute. Of the efficacy of a football tied to the back of the belt as a life-preserver I had some doubts. It seemed to me, however, that the elevation of that particular section of the anatomy could only be secured at the cost of putting the head under water. Not being quite sure, I deemed it best not to shake Joe's confidence by telling him of my doubts.

The Yellowstone divides a half mile or so above the Main Street bridge, not far from the point where Jim Cutler was knocked from his raft. The northerly channel, flowing by Livingston has perhaps a third of the volume of the southerly one. The two unite not far below the H Street bridge. In doing a bit of advance scouting down stream a day or two previously I made particular mental note of a point, just below the confluence, at which the current drove with great force close to the left bank. Here, either snags or slightly submerged boulders made a messy stretch of water that I saw at a glance it would not do to get a boat into. However, a good sharp pull across the current from the point the main channel was entered would be enough to avoid trouble—if nothing went wrong.

The currents of the respective channels came together almost at right angles, that of the main one flowing at perhaps eight miles an hour. Ordinarily I would have eased into this by running parallel to it and conforming my course to the direction of the stronger current. In my anxiety to get quick way on across the current, however, I did not take the time to do this. On the contrary, indeed, pulling as hard as I could, I drove the light skiff almost head-on into the swiftly speeding green bolt of the main current. The effect, naturally, was something like that of a man's walking into the side of a moving street car. The boat did precisely what a man walking into a car would do—went reeling and staggering sideways in an effort to keep from rolling over and over. She spun round twice before I got her under control, and of course shipped a lot of green water—all of it in Holt's section. It wasn't enough to bother much, though, and I had no trouble in pulling clear of the danger point with yards to spare. Holt went quietly to bailing. I was conscious of a mild thrill of elation at the thought of the sousing I was giving him in spite of the "doughnut," but he didn't seem to be worrying about it quite as much as I would have liked.

There was less excuse for Joe's having trouble at this point, because it was almost in his back yard—one of his favourite fishing riffles, in fact. It may be that the fact that I was crowding him closely from behind made him nose into the main channel faster than he would have done had he been on his own. I was too busy with my own troubles to see what happened to him, so could only judge from the tremolo of his high-keyed cursing. Holt, however, who had a grandstand seat for the twin performances, said that the canvas canoe was thrown just about on its beams' ends, and that nothing but the newly installed water-line air-chambers, prevented a complete swamping.

The bend below the Northern Pacific bridge was one of the two or three places of which I seemed to have retained much of a mental picture from my previous run. Twenty years before the main channel was cutting heavily into a low bluff on the left, bringing down an enormous quantity of big round boulders. The short, savage riffle formed by these had given us our first severe mauling on that earlier ride. Now I found the river had broadened greatly, pouring a shallow current through a channel two or three hundred yards wide. But it was still swift, very swift—altogether relentless in its onward urge. It is the almost complete absence of slack-water stretches that differentiates the five

95

hundred miles of the Yellowstone between Gardiner and Glendive from any other great river I can recall. It is this that makes it so nearly ideal for boating.

It didn't take us long to discover that as a pilot Joe was not an asset. Personally he was a source of never-ending delight; also artistically. His funny little craft with its inner-tube bilge keels, no less than the bobbing of that football life-preserver, lent touches to the picture that could have been blocked in by no other media. But what made Joe's piloting fail to qualify was the fact that instead of trying to find the channel he was trying to find floaters—to earn one or both of those twenty-five-dollar rewards that were offered for the finding of the bodies of the people drowned the previous week. I wanted all the deep, clear, unobstructed channel there was to be had; the very nature of Joe's quest kept him edging in toward snags and bars and shallows. These little incidentals didn't bother him a bit. The instant he saw the water shoaling dangerously he simply jumped overboard, grabbed his feather-weight craft by the nose and trotted right out on dry land.

Now this wouldn't have troubled seriously if—save the mark!—I had also been using an unladen canvas canoe. But with my outfit, a passenger, and a boat whose ability to withstand collisions with rocks and snags had still to be proved, Joe's little jump-out, pick-up and trot-off maneuver was a difficult one to follow. Twice, because there was no alternative either time, I did the best I could to go through his motions. All I succeeded in doing—besides getting pulled down and rolled—was proving that the bottom of my boat would bang for fifty feet over shallowly submerged rocks without holing. While that latter was reassuring, I couldn't see any reason for going on and proving it over and over again. If the constant drop of water wears away the hardest stone it seemed perfectly reasonable to believe that the constant biff of boulders might batter through the hardest bottom. And I wanted that bottom to do me for from twenty-five to thirty-five hundred miles yet.

That was the reason why when, entangled in a maze of shoaling channels, Joe picked up his canoe and trotted up on a bar for the third time, I had the corner of a wild-weather eye lifting for a possible gateway of escape. A short, sharp chute cascading off to the right seemed to fill the bill, but by a narrow squeeze. A rough tumble of green-white water drove full at a caving gravel bank, reared up and fell over on its back in a curling wave, serpentined between the out-reaching claws formed by the roots of two prostrate cottonwood trees, and then recovered from its tantrum in a diminuendo of whirlpools in the embrasure of a brown cliff. It was the kind of a place which you knew you could run if all went right, but which you usually didn't try for fear that one of a half dozen things might go wrong. I should hardly have tackled it in cold blood, even in a boat I was thoroughly used to; but I had just enough dander up over the prospect of another bumping on Joe's bar to be just a bit careless of consequences. It was that sort of "Might-as-well-be-hanged-for-a-sheep-as-a-lamb" feeling that a man ought to eliminate from his system as a first step in fitting himself for work in rough water. It had always troubled me a bit, but I had it sufficiently in check to keep it from asserting itself unless I was very tired or slightly huffed. This time, I fear, there was just a bare ruffle of huffiness easing the brake of my wonted restraint.

I was over the dip at the head of that chute before I knew it—likewise, out into the swirls at the foot of it. I was conscious only of a sudden dive, the loom of the back-curling wave—which the skiff, heeling half over, was taking as a racing car round a steeply-banked turn,—a tangle of roots to left and right, and then the serpentining through the whirlpools. She had hardly shipped a bucket of solid water—most of it over her bows as she tipped off the curling wave.

Joe was quite handsome above having his pilotage flaunted. The first thing he did after catching up with us was to apologize again for having warned about running the upper river. The good chap seemed really to think that some skill had been displayed in running that chute. As a matter of fact, I simply headed in and let the current do the rest. Pete said I backed water sharply to keep from ramming the gravel bank, and that we both fended with oars against the clutch of the cottonwood snags. Pete also said I was pop-eyed all the way through. I know that he was. I was glad of it, too. Outside of a straight spill, I felt that there wasn't going to be much more that I could do to shake those confoundedly cool scout-trained nerves of his.

This little incident clarified the air on the pilotage question. I let Joe keep the lead as far as I could, but assumed the responsibility of picking my own channel while he concentrated on his quest.

We passed several grim reminders of the tragedies of the past week. A few miles below Livingston we came upon Jim Cutler's raft stranded upon a midstream bar. Even a passing glimpse revealed how well the double tiers of logs were laid—plainly the work of the real old river-rat "Buckskin Jim" must have been. Not far below the raft was the wreck of a Ford, with cushions, wraps, and odds and ends of a camp outfit dotting the bars for the next mile or two. The car, occupied by a young Middle Westerner and his four-months' bride, had gone over the grade at a bend of the road not far above where we saw the wreck. Rolling to the flood-swollen river, it had been carried several hundred yards down stream before stranding. The man crawled clear and reached the bank; the body of his wife had not been recovered. The third recent river tragedy was that of a rancher, but I had not learned the details of it.

I was, of course, much elated over the way in which my little tin boat had behaved in running that side-winding chute. This very smart performance proved conclusively that, with anything like intelligent handling, she would be more than equal to any probable demands I would have to make on her. There might, of course, be places that I would have to avoid on account of her lack of freeboard, but that, at the worst, would mean no more than the loss of a bit of time. She was good for what she would have to do—that was the main thing. There was reassurance, also, in the way her bottom and sides had withstood the bumping from the rocks. There was no question in my mind now that that galvanized tin-like looking stuff was real steel. Nothing else would have stood the bumps. I planned to spare her all that kind of thing I could, but it was good to know that she could stand the gaff if she had to. I was calling her pet names before we had gone twenty miles. It is an astonishing thing the affection a man develops for a boat that is carrying him well on a long river journey.

The thing that I remembered best from my former run was the long, rough rapid that winds down and under the Springdale bridge. I did not recall, however, that the river divided into two channels a half mile above the bridge. Indeed, it is quite possible that it did not do so twenty years ago. Changes like that occur over night during the high-water season on the Yellowstone. Joe led the way down the left-hand side of the left-hand channel, but landed when it became apparent that neither of our boats could live in the wild tumble of rollers where the current drove hard against the side of the bluff above the bridge. Lining back a quarter of a mile up-stream, we pulled across to the opposite side, down which there was rough but fairly open running.

My boat was behaving so well that I couldn't resist the temptation to give her a baptism in some really rough stuff at a point where salvage operations would be so comparatively simple in case of grief. Giving the little lady her head after the worst of the riffle had been passed, I let the undercurrent draw her right over into the main string of rollers. Wild, wallowing water it was, solid white all the way, but with a straight run and no underhand look about it. She took it like a duck, except where two or three of the most broken combers let her down too sharply for her bows to rise to meet the next in turn. There were perhaps a half dozen buckets of water in the forward section when we beached and dumped her a hundred yards below the bridge. As I seem to remember it now, Syd Lamartine's skiff had a foot of water in it when we dumped at about the same point on that other run. On that occasion, however, I have a clear recollection of riding the middle of the riffle all the way down. I should want a batteau and a full crew if I were going to try the same stunt today.

It must have been six or seven miles below the Springdale bridge that Holt, descrying an unusual object on the beach of a long, low island to our left, asked me to pull in closer for a better look. Joe, a hundred yards ahead of us, had already passed it up as a log of driftwood, but the ex-scout's keen eye would not be deceived. At first we thought it was the body of a man—probably the drowned rancher,—but as we drew nearer it was revealed as that of a woman dressed in hiking garb, undoubtedly the bride of the auto wreck.

As we were now in Sweet Grass County, the body was under the jurisdiction of the Coroner at Big Timber. Holt decided it would be best if Joe tried to find some ranch from which he could get in touch with that official by phone, while we continued on down river to carry the word by an alternative route.

Joe was treated to a good deal of a shock while towing the body downstream to an eddy from which it could be landed on the left bank. No sooner had he put off from the beach than the corpse, floating deeply submerged at the end of a thirty-foot line, made straight for the roaring line of rollers on the right side of the channel. As it was a good deal too rough water for his boat to ride, Joe lost no time in bending to his stubby oars and pulling for dear life in the opposite direction. It was a tug-of-war all the way, with the grisly tow on the outer end gaining foot by foot. Holt and I had drifted too far ahead before we realized the seriousness of Joe's difficulty to be of any help. As an upset was inevitable in the event the canoe was dragged into the riffle stern first, the best that we could do was to pick him up at the foot of it and trust that his canoe would strand and anchor the corpse.

If that riffle had been fifty yards longer nothing in the world could have prevented a spill that would have put Joe's football life-preserver to a real test. As far as the tug-of-war was concerned he was beaten completely—dragged over the line. Luckily it was only the smoothening tail of the riffle, and the buoyant little canoe rode the rounded rollers without capsizing. Another hundred yards, and the relentless drag from the other end of his line had eased enough to allow him to pull up and into the eddy. He was mighty white about the gills as Holt gave him a hand ashore, and kept repeating over and over in an awed voice: "Did you see her try to drown me? Did you see her try to drown me?"

It was easy enough to understand what the trouble had been as soon as one gave it a moment's collected thought. Calm reflection, however, was a thing which I am inclined to think very few men would have been capable of in Joe's place. As a matter of fact, indeed, neither Holt nor I was in a sufficiently detached frame of mind to dope out the phenomenon until some minutes after Joe had landed. This was the reason for what happened:

In every swiftly flowing channel there is a strong draw toward the most rapidly moving part of the current, and this draw is usually more powerful below than at the surface. A boat paddled in comparatively smooth water beside a riffle will invariably be drawn into the latter within a few yards if allowed to drift. Only too often, in fact, it will be drawn in despite every effort to avoid the riffle. In this particular instance, the deeply floating corpse had given the inward drawing current a double hold, and Joe's short oars had not been able to develop power enough to counteract it. Readily explicable as the uncanny incident was, there was no question of the grim seriousness of it. Indeed, I have always thought of it as a battle with Death in more senses than one, for that football float of Joe's, attached as it was, would have been about as much use as a life-preserver, once he was dumped out into that riffle, as a millstone round his neck.

Holt and I made good time for the remainder of the run to Big Timber—about three hours for something like twenty-five miles. The way was a continuous succession of moderate rapids, with one very rough and savage cascade. The latter was not far above Big Timber, and was formed by a ledge of bedrock extending all the way across the river. A direct drop of two or three feet here was followed by a series of stiff riffles that extended out of sight round a sharp bend where the river was deflected at right-angles by an abrupt cliff. I never learned the name of the place, but it was a distinctly nasty one—just one damn thing after another, as Pete put it. I have jumbled memories of messing up on the ledge, and then half swamping just below it, on my former run.

Not to take too many chances in the deepening twilight (though all we'd admit to each other at the time was that we were doing it to avoid wetting my outfit), we lined by the sharp pitch and on down almost to the bend. Even from there it was right sloppy going, partly through some rather clumsy handling the skiff had as a consequence of a sudden divergence of theory Pete and I developed on the subject of rapid running.

Rounding the sharp bend the skiff was drawn into the middle of a rough, foam-white riffle that extended ahead as far as I could see. The unrhythmically wallowing rollers were banging her bows unmercifully and throwing water aboard at a rate that I feared would swamp her very quickly if she continued to head into them. Seeing that the water toward the right bank was a bit less broken, I laid onto my oars for all that was in me in an effort to throw her in that direction. Holt was grunting mightily. Looking ahead over my shoulder, I could not see what he was doing, but assumed he was paddling his head off in seconding my effort to reach smoother water. But not a yard could I move her from the crest of that white-capped ridge of rollicking combers. Down the whole length of the riffle she slammed, dipping water at every plunge and finishing with a good six inches swishing about in both sections.

Just about at the last gasp from my frantic but futile pulling, I let my oars trail and my head sag down between my knees while my heart stopped hop-skip-and-a-jumping and my breath came back. Looking up a half minute later to see if there was anything ahead that would demand expert attention, I saw that Pete was just coming out of a collapse similar to my own. Also he was choking toward utterance.

"Took all I had in me,—but I did it," he gasped with a sickly grin.

"Did what?" I growled.

"Kept you from throwing her side-on and giving me that spill you promised," he chuckled. "Don't you think it's getting too late in the evening for that kind of jokes?"

Oh, well! The warehouses and the water-tanks of the Big Timber bluff were beginning to blot the evening sky ahead, and so I hardly thought it worthwhile to explain to Pete that his fancied self-defensive measures had probably brought him nearer to that promised spill than he had been at any time during the day. He wouldn't have believed me anyhow. Won't even do so when he reads it here in cold print.

Pulling up a slough that ran back from the head of the bluff, we found safe haven under the over-arching willows of a wonderfully cold and clear little creek. Pushing out onto the bank above, we found ourselves in the back yard of the local postmaster. A highly gracious and comely young lady volunteered to mend my Gieve waistcoat, torn by Pete's frantic paddlings over and roundabout the inflated "doughnut." The Gieve is not made to paddle in.

Wolfing great porterhouse steaks and quaffing steaming mugs of coffee, Pete and I sat long at a lunch-counter table and talked of our ancient ski jaunt over the snows of the Yellowstone. He spoke much of coasting and jumping and spills—especially of spills that I took. Just why he did this didn't occur to me until after he had left for Livingston by the midnight train. I figured it out walking back to the hotel. It was merely the subtle chap's way of letting me know that he still reckoned I was a bit in his debt on the score of thrills and spills. Maybe so. Maybe so. Twenty-year thrills more readily than forty-year, just as forty-year is more reluctant to take a chance at a spill.

HBC officials in an express canoe, 1825

IV - BIG TIMBER TO BILLINGS

A troop of round-up artists jingled into Big Timber the morning of July first, just as I was leaving the hotel to go down to my boat. They were in from the ranges on their way to compete at the annual cow-carnival at Miles City. Having read of my voyage in the paper, they came to me with the proposal that I book the lot of them as passengers. They assumed that I would easily make the two hundred and fifty mile run in a day, and that my boat had unlimited cabin capacity. I replied by inviting them down to my moorings. The sight of the tiny tin shallop tied up under the willows brought them to a more reasonable view of the situation. They readily admitted that it would not carry anything like ten people, even without their saddles, but they were inclined to argue that it would carry at least four besides myself.

I assured them I was game to try it if they were, but suggested that the four elected should get in first. Now four light-footed sailors might have stepped into that little boat and taken their seats without upsetting it. Four booted and spurred cow-punchers could not, or at least did not. In fact the third one precipitated the swamping when he stumbled and fell over the two who had preceded him. After we had raised, dumped and launched her again, I assured them that a single passenger was my outside limit, but that I would be highly honoured by the company of any one of them whom they would agree to nominate for the run to Billings. As I was planning to stop over a day or two there, my arrival by river in Miles would be too late for the opening of the Round-up.

After some debate they picked the "bulldogger" of the outfit. "Bull-dogging" is a stock round-up stunt, and I shall hardly need to explain that the modus operandi involves throwing a steer by seizing its nose in the teeth and upsetting its centre of gravity by a sudden twist of the neck. One sees it in every rodeo, but it is a feat withal that requires much nerve, strength and skill.

Jocularly remarking that he reckoned he would have to ride this tin broncho with a slick heel, the "dogger" unbuckled his spurs and stepped into the boat. I went up to fetch my remaining bags from the postmaster's house and was delayed ten minutes while the stitching up of my Gieve was completed. When I returned I found a bewhiskered stranger recounting with facile gesture how he fished the floaters out of the eddy below his ranch down-river. He called it "Dead Man's Douse." Last floater he took out was a cow-puncher who had been so rolled in the big rapid above that his spurs were tangled in his hair and he came wheeling through the suds like a doughnut. It was a hells-bells-jingler of a rapid, that one above the "Douse." Water tossed about so fierce that the fishes' brains were spattered on the rocks!

That was about all I arrived in time to hear, but the "dogger" had been more fortunate. The good chap was deeply impressed, too, for his iron, bull-nose-biting jaw was sagging in a sickly grin and he was back on the bank offering a free passage to Billings to any of his mates who cared to accept. No takers. The gamest of the lot appeared to be a lady broncho-buster called Lil. She actually stepped into the boat once, but finally decided to take the train because it had a roof on it. It looked like rain, she said, and it always made her broken shoulder ache to get wet. As if rain was the wettest part of riding the Yellowstone.

Just as I was about to push off the whiskered rancher stepped up and asked if I minded giving him a bit of a down-river lift. Gladly I bade him come along, figuring that his pilotage would give me a better chance of avoiding the dreaded "Douse." The round-up artists sped us with their college yell as I crabbed out of the little slough to the river. I bumped into some of them again in Miles the day after the Round-up. Most of their faces bore the marks of hoof or fist. Lady Lil had lost no cuticle (at least where it showed), but red eyes hoisted the distress signal of a deeper seated wound. The "dogger" had taken up with another girl—a she-dude that had once been a bare-back rider in a circus. Lil had been crying a lot, which was no end of a shame considering how wetness affected her busted shoulder. All of which went to prove that Lilly the Lady Broncho-Buster and Judy O'Grady were sisters under the skin. And Lil had looked so darned exempt from the surge of the soft stuff!

There is a fairly rough riffle just below the Big Timber, and then a lot of rather mean navigating through the shallows where the boulders of Clark's famous "Rivers Across" litter the channel of the Yellowstone. The whiskered stranger, stroking with an oar from the stern, was of real help in making the passage of both comparatively quiet and dry. He also found me a smooth-running strip of green through the almost solid tumble of white where the river was chasing its tail in a sharply notched bend about five miles farther on. These little riffles didn't bother me much, though. My mind was too much occupied by the "Dead Man's Douse" for that. I was wondering whether the old chap intended to run me through that fish-brain-spattering-rapid, or if he might be considerate enough to help me portage round. I was trying to get my nerve up to broaching the latter procedure when my pilot dug hard with his steering oar and brought the skiff up to a gravelly landing below a pretty little tree-covered bench. His cabin was back behind the bull-berries, he said, and he would have to leave me here. Or perhaps I would hang on for an hour and have some coffee and a mess of sinkers with him.

"But aren't you going to see me through the Dead Man's Douse?" I exclaimed in dismay, adding in a feeble attempt at funniness: "It might save you fishing out my remains later."

A corner of the tobacco-stained mouth drew out in a highly amused chuckle. "By jingo, sonny," he giggled finally, "it wasn't youse I was shootin' for with that yarn. I thought youse savvied all the time. I jest was wantin' this here seat that bull-biting cow-puncher had perempted. There ain't no 'Dead Man's Douse.' Fack is, youse got most of the sloppy stuff ahint youse already. Don't get too gosh-all-fired sure of you'self an' youse all right—tin boat an' all."

It was with real regret that the threat of coming storm made it necessary for me to keep going while I could. The good old chap had made casual mention of Terry and Miles and Gibbon, of hunting buffalo and elk on the river in the early days, and of many comparatively recent jaunts down the Yellowstone searching for agates. He would have been well worth listening to. I never learned his name, but I have always thought of him as "Jim Bridger"—because he lied with so classic a simplicity, painting his pictures as—well, as a river paints its rocks with fish-brains!

There were a good half dozen sinister-cloaked thunder-storms doing their war dances in this direction or that as I left "Jim Bridger" and pushed back into the stream. The wolf-fanged Crazies to the north were getting the liveliest of them, but there were also some tremendous disturbances going on among the snowy pinnacles where the Absarokas reared against the southern sky. The restlessly counter-marching clouds above the valley were full of whirling wind-gusts but not of rain. The sudden side-swipes of air kept the skiff yawing rather crazily, but as there was no very fine shooting to do for the moment I kept going. Indeed, I was quite unconcerned about the threat of the weather. I still had to learn a proper respect for thunder-storms—the same very wholesome kind of respect that I had for really rough water. That was to come in good time, and by the usual channel—experience, very vivid experience.

I had not yet come to the point on the river where Clark had built and launched his dugout. Constantly searching for suitable timber, he had skirted the northern bank closely all the way down from where he had first come to the Yellowstone near the present site of Livingston. The flint-paved mesas wore down the hoofs of his Indian ponies so that it became necessary to protect them with shoes of buffalo hide. This increased Clark's anxiety to take to the river and his diary speaks often of the vain search for large trees. Very near the point I had now reached an accident occurred which eventually forced Clark's hand and probably resulted in his constructing his boats farther up river, and from less satisfactory material, than would otherwise have been the case. The incident was picturesquely commemorated in a name borne by a certain creek upon the earlier maps.

In the vicinity of the creek in question, Clark tells how one of his men, Gibson, in mounting his horse after shooting a deer, "fell on a snag and runt (ran) it nearly two inches into the muskeler (muscular) part of his thy (thigh)." That incident inspired Clark, who had already used up the names of the members of his party a half dozen times over in geographical nomenclature, to call the creek "Thy Snag'd." Gibson suffered so much from the jolting of the horse upon which he was carried after his injury that it became necessary to rest him in camp. With a halt of two or three days imperative in any case, Clark sought out the best brace of trees in the vicinity and set his men making dugouts. Two of these, lashed together side by side, made a craft of such water-worthiness that it was not abandoned until long after the junction with Lewis on the Missouri.

Although the names given by Clark on his voyage down the Yellowstone have survived better than have most of those applied by the explorers in other regions, several of the most picturesque have not stood the test of time and chance. Shield's River, Pryor's Fork and Clark's Fork still bear their original names, but Thy Snag'd Creek and River Across are no more. The former has become Deer Creek and the latter pair have been given individual names—that flowing in from the north Big Timber Creek, that from the south Boulder River. No more original and distinctive dual nomenclature for streams flowing into a river on opposite sides of the same point could have been imagined. It is a pity that, in the nature of the case, it could not fill the nomenclatural exigency sufficiently to survive.

Fortunately for me the peculiar meteorological conditions of the morning did not develop along what I subsequently learned was their normal course at that time of year. Ordinarily a pow-wow of thunder-storms in the mountain-top in the morning means a concerted attack upon the valley in the afternoon. This time the advent of a warm south-erly wind modified the assault-and-battery program and brought only a drizzling rain on the river. The broken piers of Greycliff's ruined bridge menaced me from the mist as I drove past, and below the new bridge the sagging strand of a slackened cable swooped at me from the air. Then came a sharp bend, with the roar of a considerable rapid booming in the grey obscurity below. The rain and the mist deadened the sound somewhat, just as they confused the perspective. Standing up on the thwart in an endeavour to get a better view, I was warned by the accel-erating undulations of the skiff that I had floated right onto the intake of a riffle which I had assumed was still several hundred yards distant. Hastening to straighten the cushion on my seat before taking to my oars, I was jolted from my feet by the first solid wave, so that I sat with my full weight upon the doubled-up index finger of my left hand. I distinctly recall either hearing or feeling the snap of what I thought at the moment was a tendon, but as the finger still crooked with its fellow round its oar I gave it no more thought until I had slammed through to quieter water, a quarter of a mile below. Then I found the finger was bent inward to the resemblance of a rather open letter C. Taking it for granted it was dislocated, I started and kept on pulling it until another riffle demanded personal attention. Always afraid to take it to a doctor for fear of being held up, at gradually increasing intervals I kept on trying to pull that drooping pointer into place for the next two months. It was in St. Louis that I found that two bones had been broken in the first place, and that they had probably been re-broken every time I pulled the finger afterwards. It is not quite back to shape yet, which, everything considered, is hardly to be wondered at.

A lifting of the mist accompanied an increase in the rain, with the balance inclining toward a better visibility. This latter came opportunely, for the loom of high cliffs on the right and a running close of the rounded hills on the left seemed to indicate a canyon and bad water. It was an agreeable surprise to find only a straight, swift reach of river bordered with a narrow belt of cottonwood on either side. There appeared no menace of mist-masked rapids ahead, but with the rain settling into what seemed likely to be an all-day downpour I was glad to pull up to the left bank where an enchanting vista of ranch buildings opened up beneath the cottonwoods. The tree I tied up to had a trunk fully four feet in diameter, and I was puzzled to account for the fact that Clark had overlooked it in his search for boat timber—until it occurred to me that the grey-barked giant was perhaps a bit smaller with a hundred and sixteen fewer annual rings on it.

There are a number of pleasing little things that happen to the voyageur by the Running Road, but not many that awaken a warmer glow in his sodden breast than stepping almost direct from a wet boat into a kitchen fragrant with the ineffable sweetness of frying doughnuts. And when the doughnuts are being forked forth by an astonishingly comely and kindly young housewife; and when her husband comes in from the alfalfa patch and proves just as kindly if less comely; and when they insist on your drying out and staying to dinner and then—because the rain still continues—to supper and all night; and when the three of you sit up till all hours and tell each other everything you ever did—and how—and why: well, all that just makes it nicer still.

They were a sterling pair of young pioneers, these Fahlgrens. Both were from Kentucky. He had come out to Montana about ten years before and homesteaded what he reckoned as the loveliest spot on the whole Yellowstone. A little later he had made a hurried trip home to bring back a young woman that he reckoned just as lovely and just as promising as his ranch. Neither had disappointed him. His ranch had doubled and trebled in size, with his family just about keeping pace with it. There were hard years behind, with not any too easy sledding at the present; but there had been much happiness all along the road and the future was bright with promise. How heartening it was even to brush in passing such kindliness, simplicity, hopefulness and courage!

We had Maryland fried chicken and a big golden pone of corn bread for breakfast. All left over was put up for my lunch, together with a gooseberry pie. As the early morning weather was still fitful and showery, I did not start until ten o'clock, taking Fahlgren with me for a couple of miles to the next down-river ranch. He wanted me to drift a rapid stern-first, as the agate hunters were wont to do it. Trimmed as we were, I knew what must happen. I agreed to the trial readily enough, however, partly because it was Fahlgren's suggestion but principally because it was he, and not I, that was sitting in the stern. Riding so low, the after section shipped a dozen bucketfuls of green water, all of it via my passenger's knees. The riffle was not rough enough to make any real trouble, and we both took the thing strictly in a larking spirit.

One can drift a riffle stern first that is too rough to ride any other way. Facing down-stream, and pulling against the current the headway of the boat is checked and it is easier to shoot it to right or left to avoid an obstacle. If the riffle is not too rough to make the control of the boat impossible when rowed bow-first with the stream, drifting means the cutting down of speed and the loss of much good time. Also, a boat one is going to use for drifting should have a stout, high stern (whether double-ended or not) and temporarily at least, it should be lightened aft and trimmed to ride well down by the head.

Not long after I had parted with Fahlgren a distinct change in the weather took place. The charged, humid thunderstorm condition of the atmosphere gave way to sharp, keen north-westerly weather. A strong wind became a stronger, and by noon the valley was swept by a whistling gale blowing straight from the main western mass of the Rockies. The fact that it was almost dead astern as the general course of the river ran was the only thing that made keeping on the water a thing to be considered at all. An equally strong gale blowing up-stream would have tried to stand the river on its head and scoop the channel dry. It would have succeeded in neither, but the resulting rough-and-tumble would have kicked up a wild welter of white caps such as no skiff could have lived in for half a minute. But with current and wind going in the same general direction it was quite another matter, especially as I had a chance to ease up to it gradually as the gale increased in force. I was making such tremendous headway, and the spell of the wild ride was so strong in my blood, that my wonted cautiousness was swamped in a rising tide of exhilaration. There are few who will not have experienced the feeling of being intoxicated with swift air and rapid motion. It was more than that with me this time. I was inebriated—stewed—loaded to the guards. I was having the time of my young life and I hadn't the least intention of going home until morning.

Now in real life a man who starts out in such a state of exaltation always bangs up against some immovable body good and hard before he is through. Or, more properly speaking, his getting through is more or less coincident with his banging against such a body. Why something like that didn't put a period to my mad career on this occasion has never been clear in my mind. Possibly that more or less mythical Providence that has been known (though by no means often enough to warrant the proverb) to shepherd drunks and fools had something to do with it. At any rate, I was still in mad career down midstream when the wind gave up the bootless chase at six o'clock, broke up into fitful zephyrs and went to sleep among the cottonwoods. In all that time I had not landed once, had not relinquished both oars for a single second, and had not even munched my Maryland fried chicken and gooseberry pie. Skippers have stood longer watches, but never a one has carried on with less relief. On that score, perhaps, I may have deserved to win through. On every other count I was going out of my way to ask for trouble and had nothing but my lucky star to thank for having avoided it.

I passed Reed Point and Columbus early in the afternoon. Beyond the latter point I began keeping watch for a certain long line of bluffs which I knew began near the railway station called Rapids and extended easterly for three miles. Clark had called them "Black Bluffs," and that name they retain to this day, though their only claim to blackness even in Clark's time came from the presence of dark green undergrowth. Today they are brown and comparatively bare.

I picked up the rounded sky-line of "Black Bluffs" at just about the time that the straight, hard-running riffle that gives Rapids Station its name began to boom ahead. The middle of the riffle was plainly no place for a little tin shallop, but down the right side there appeared to be fairly open channel. Settling that course in my mind, I let the tail of my eye steal back to the head of the bluff, and from there to a cottonwood covered flat that opened up beyond the bend where the river, thrown off a ledge of bedrock, turned sharply to the south in a stolid stream of rock-torn white. Beyond question there was going to be some fairly nice navigation demanded to find a way through that rough stuff below the bend, especially as the wind was going to come strongly abeam for a short distance. All of which was hard luck, I complained to myself, for the end of that line of bluffs pointed an unerring finger at the flat below them as the place where Clark had halted, built his boats and taken to the river. I had hoped for a better look at it than I saw I was going to get.

Even the pressing exigencies of the navigational problem could not quite obliterate from my mind the realization of the fact that—from some point not more than a few insignificant hundreds of yards ahead—Captain William Clark was going to be my pilot all the way to St. Louis. Exulting over that wasn't what was at the bottom of the trouble, however. You can tread a lot of highways and byways of fancy without seriously impairing your river navigation, but only when you keep your eyes on the water and the back of your mind in a proper state to receive impressions and transmit orders. I was not in the least culpable in this respect. The reason I hit that mid-stream snag was because a sudden hail from some men grading a road over the bluff caused just enough of a congestion of my ganglionic lines to slow down proper and adequate action. I checked by an effort the impulse to cup a hand to an ear in an attempt to catch the import of what was doubtless a warning of some sort, but as a consequence failed to get through in time the order for my left hand to back its oar when the imminent snag bobbed up.

The skiff struck on her starboard bow, slid along the snag for a few feet, and then swung and hung there, side-on to the current and the wind. White water dashed in over the up-stream gunwale and mingled with green water poured over the down-stream. But just before the forces from above threw her completely on her beams-ends the flexible root bent down and let her swing off without capsizing. It was a merry dance to the bend, but I managed to get her under control in time to head into the best of the going through the suds below. This was close to the right bank, where I had no little trouble in holding her on account of the side-surge from the heavy west wind. This is not a hard series of riffles to run if you have no bad luck, but an upset in the upper riffle would leave you at the mercy of the lower, which is a savage tumble of combers filling most of the channel. In that respect this double riffle below Rapids Station is a good deal like the combination of Rock Slide and Death Rapids on the Big Bend of the Columbia. The latter pair are, however, incomparably the rougher.

I was a mile away and on the farther side of the valley before I got rid of enough water to survey for damages. A long, jagged scratch down the side, with a big, round dent at the point of first impact, were the only marks she showed of the collision. Light as was the steel, it had not come near to holing from a blow that stopped her dead from at least twelve miles an hour. This renewed assurance of the staunchness of my tight little tin pan was by no means unwelcome. There would still be a lot of things to bump into, even after leaving the Yellowstone.

My only mental picture of the site of Clark's shipyard was that received from the one hurried glance as I came to the upper rapid. There was no chance for a second look. Sentimentally I was sorry not to have been able to land and pretend to look for the stumps of the trees cut down for the dugouts. As a matter of fact, however, as the river had been altering its channel every season for over a hundred years, there was no question in my mind but that the shipyard flat had been made and washed out a score of times since Clark was there.

Captain Clark's party spent four days building the two dugout canoes and exploring in this vicinity. Twenty-four of their horses were stolen by Indians and never recovered. The same fate ultimately overtook the remainder of the bunch, which Sergeant Pryor and two others were attempting to drive overland to the Mandan villages on the Missouri. Clark described the canoes as "twenty-eight feet long, sixteen or eighteen inches deep and from sixteen to twenty-four inches wide." Lashed together, these must have made a clumsy but very serviceable craft. Considering its weight and type, their first-day run in it—from Rapids to the mouth of Pryor's Fork, near Huntley—strikes me as being a remarkable one. The Captain's actual estimates of distances on this part of his journey are much too high and also present many discrepancies. This particular run, however, is easy fixable by natural features. It must be very close to sixty miles as the river winds, possibly more. It is not fair to compare this with the considerably faster time I made over similar stretches of the Yellowstone. I had considerably higher and swifter water and a boat so light that no delays from shallows and bars were imposed. Very generally speaking, I found my rate of travel on the Yellowstone to have worked out about twenty-five per cent. faster than that of Clark's party. On the Missouri, on stretches where I did not use my outboard motor, I averaged just about the same as the united explorers on their down-stream voyage. There is little doubt that they stopped longer and oftener than I did on the Missouri, and that while on the river their big crews snatched along whatever type of craft they happened to be manning at a considerably faster rate than I pulled. By and large, however, I should say that Kipling's

"Down to Gehenna or up to the Throne,

He travels the fastest who travels alone,"

holds quite as good on the Running Road as in Life's Handicap.

In the journal of the first day on the river Captain Clark writes: "At the distance of a mile from camp the river passes under a high bluff for about 23 miles, when the bottom widens on both sides." This would give the impression that the river flowed continuously for many miles under an overhanging bluff. This it does not do, and could hardly have done at any previous period. What it does do is to run along the base of a long chain of broken bluffs, many of which it has undermined. I have always thought of this as by long odds the most beautiful and picturesque stretch of stream I navigated between the Rockies and the lower Mississippi.

The bluffs varied in natural colour from a grey-brown to a reddish-black, but mosses and lichens and mineral stains from the hills behind tinted their abrupt faces with streaks and patches of various shades, all blended like delicate pastelling. The main stream usually ran close up against the bluffs, but numerous chutes and back-channels sprawling over the verdant flats to the left formed score on score of small islands, all shaded with tall cottonwoods, lush with new grass and brilliant with wild flowers. There was a fresh vista of beauty at every turn. It was a shame not to be able to stop and call on the Queen of the Fairies. Titania's Bowers succeeded each other like apartments on upper Broadway. For the second time that day I regretted my speed and the fact that wind and rough water kept my attention riveted close to the boat.

At first I gave the face of the bluffs a wide berth, especially at those points where the full strength of the current went swirling beneath the painted overhang in sinuous coils of green and white. As I think of it now, it was the cavernous growls and rumbles, magnified by the sounding board of the cliff, that made me chary of venturing in where the animals were being fed. The racket was not a little terrifying until one found that it was more bark than bite.

It was not until a sudden side-swiping squall forced me under an overhang I was doing my best to avoid that I had direct and conclusive evidence that the yawning mouths had no teeth in them. Swift as it was, the surface of the water was untorn by lurking rocks, while the refluent waves from the inner depths of the cavern had a tendency to force the boat out rather than to draw it in. My courage rallied rapidly after that, so that I played hide-and-seek with the river and the cliffs for the next twenty miles. This was most opportune, as it chanced. The overhangs provided me with cover from the worst of a heavy series of rain squalls that began to sweep the river at this juncture, and continued for an hour or more. All in all, that little bluff-bluffing stunt proved one of the most novel and delightful bits of boating I have ever known.

I passed the mouth of Clark's Fork a little before six. Its channel was much divided by gravel bars, and the comparatively small streams might easily have been mistaken for returning back-chutes of the Yellowstone. Clark had at first mistaken this river for the Big Horn, and only applied his own name to it when the greater tributary was reached some hundred and fifty miles below. I scooped up a drink as I passed one of the mouths. Clark's observation that it was colder and cloudier than the waters of the Yellowstone still held good. Clark mentions a "ripple in the Yellowstone" about a mile above this tributary, "on passing which the canoes took in some water. The party therefore landed to bail the boats...." As this, considering the size of the boats, would have indicated very rough water, I kept a close watch for the place. I never located it definitely, though sharp riffles were numerous all the way. Doubtless parts of the channel have altered completely since Clark's time. As a rule, however, rapids change less with the years than the opener stretches—this because they are usually made by bedrock or boulders of great size.

I made my first landing since dropping Fahlgren at a flower-embowered farmhouse not far below the mouth of Clark's Fork. All of the family were away except a very motherly old lady who had just received word by phone from Billings that Dempsey had licked Carpentier. She had draped the Stars and Stripes over the porch railing and insisted that I stop and celebrate the great national victory with her. I demurred, but my resolution weakened when she began setting out a pan of scarcely diluted cream, a bowl of strawberries and a chocolate cake. Between mouthfuls I told her (truthfully enough) that I had met Carpentier at the Front during the war and had subsequently seen him box in London. It was a tactical error on my part. I should have known better. She didn't tell me to back away from the berries in so many words, but her manner changed, and she did say that it was too bad it was not Dempsey I had met instead of the Frenchie. That didn't spoil my appetite for the strawberries and cream, but it did make me more conservative in my relations with them. I probably stopped short by two or three helpings of my capacity. It is not fair to one's self to be bound by the rigid limitations of truthfulness when trying to impress strangers. I resolved not to make that mistake again.

Water had been unusually high all along the Yellowstone during the early summer rise, the crest of which was now over by about a fortnight. The discharge from Clark's Fork had been especially heavy, and the effects of this I began to encounter as soon as I resumed my run to Billings. Scores of new channels had been scoured out and countless thousands of big cottonwoods and willows uprooted in the process. Most of the latter were stranded on shallow bars, but every now and then some great giant had anchored itself squarely in mid-channel. It took no end of care to avoid them, and it was a distinct relief to find that the wind had now fallen very light.

My old strawberry lady had estimated the distance to Billings as about twenty miles, but such was the extreme deviousness of the endlessly divided channels that it must have been greatly in excess of that. One minute I would be in what was undoubtedly the main channel. The next I would be picking what seemed the likeliest of four or five sprawling chutes, with whichever one I took usually dividing and redividing until I found myself scraping through the shallows and all but grounded.

With no town in sight as eight o'clock began to usher in the long midsummer twilight, I landed near a large farmhouse on the left bank to make inquiries. The buildings were fine and modern and the irrigated acres of great richness, but the people turned out to be Russian tenants, and not much for the softer things of life. All of the dozen or more occupants of the big kitchen wore bib overalls, the bottoms puckered in with a zouave-trousers effect. All were barefooted. The father and mother wore shirts. For the rest, including the grown children, the only garments were the comfortable and adequate overalls. Left to himself, the simple moujik hits upon some very practical ideas.

Save the broad, kindly Slavic faces, the only Russian thing I saw about the place was a samovar, and I sipped a mug of tea from this peacefully purring old friend while I endeavoured to find out whether any of them knew anything of the whereabouts of a certain Montana metropolis called Billings. They appeared to be trying to assure me that they had heard of such a place, and there also seemed to be some unanimity on the score of its being somewhere down river. But just how far it was by river they couldn't get together on, and even if they had had any real knowledge of the course of the stream they appeared not to have the language to express it. Certainly an estimate in versts wasn't going to help a lot. As I thanked them and turned to go the whole family trooped down to the landing to see me off. Pointing eastward to the low line of a distant bluff one of the boys delivered himself of a laconic "Dam—lookout!" I assured him I had already been warned of the dam of the local power company, and would be keeping just that kind of a good lookout for it. That gave them their cue. They were all ejaculating or registering "Dam—good—lookout!" as the current bore me away into the deepening dusk.

That last half-hour's run was an intensely trying one, though I was never in serious trouble any of the time. I kept going wrong on channels every few minutes, with the result that I found every now and then that the Yellowstone had gone off and left me on a streak of wet rocks and gravel. With a heavy boat I should have been marooned for the night a dozen times, but it was never very difficult to drag my little tin shallop on to where there was enough water trickling to lead the way back to the main channel. When an increasing frequency of lights indicated I was nearing the outskirts of a town I found the current to be running so swiftly along what appeared to be a levee on the left bank that a landing was rather too precarious to risk in the dark. I was skirting the bank for a favourable eddy when the rounding of a densely wooded bend brought me out into a stretch of slackening water directly above the dam. The long-striven-for bluff appeared to rise abruptly from the water on my right, while on my left there was a stretch of gravel bar running back to a strip of trees and the levee.

The roar of the dam was not the less impressive after bouncing off the bluff on its way to my ears, and I took no more time than was necessary to pull in and land upon the white stretch of beach. As rain was still threatening I decided to seek the town for shelter. Dragging the skiff well above high-water mark, I stacked my stuff in it, shouldered my packsack and climbed the levee. After an hour's bootless wanderings in the sloughs beyond I came back and followed the levee a half mile down-stream to the power-house below the dam. And so to town.

Suppering at a convenient lunch-counter, I drank copiously of coffee from the steaming urn at my elbow. Now of all of the drinks of the ancient and modern world that I have known, lunch-counter coffee has always proved the most inebriating. That was why I was impelled to fare forth to the prizefight bulletin boards seeking low companionship, and that must have been why I put the French on "Carpenter," and why I tried to affect vulgar ringside jargon.

"Kar-pon-tee-ayh K. O.-ed, huh?" I grunted familiarly, lounging up to a knot of local sports discussing pugilistic esoterics before the newspaper window. For an instant the jabbering ceased—just long enough for the half dozen technical experts to sweep my mud-spattered khaki with scathing glances, snort and get under way again. Only one of them was polite enough to say: "No savee Crow talkee," adding to a companion: "Indian policeman—Crow Reservation—funny don't talk 'Merican."

That certainly was not a good start. On the contrary, indeed, it was a perfectly rotten one. Which fact only makes me more proud of the resiliency of spirit I showed in coming right back and assuring them that I was not a Crow Indian, that I did talk 'Merican, and that I had been one of Jack Dempsey's first sparring partners. There was coffee-inspired artistry, too, in the inconsequentiality with which I added: "Gave Jack the K. O. once myself. Sort of a flivver ... but knocked him cold just the same."

Dear little old Strawberry Lady, didn't I swear I wouldn't forget the lesson you taught me? That made them take notice of course. For an instant they hung in the balance, searching my scarred and battered visage with awed, troubled eyes. Then dawning wonder replaced doubt in their faces, and they fell—my way. "Darn'd if you don't look the part," said one. "My name's Allstein—in hardware line—Shake!" And then they all introduced themselves like that—each with his name and line. I forget just what my name was, but it must have been something like "Spud" Gallagher. Sparring partners never vary greatly from that model of nomenclature.

Finally we retired to a pool-room, where I reminisced to an ever augmenting audience. Alas! and yet Alack-a-day! If it had only been the good old cow-town Billings of those delectable baseball days of twenty years ago, what wouldn't have been mine that night! But it was not bad as it was; not bad at all. I forget just where we were when dawn came, but I do remember I was in the act of showing my punch-damaged hands for the hundredth time when I looked up and saw that a window was growing a glimmering square with the light of the coming day. That was my cue, of course. Excusing myself on some pretext, I slipped out the back way, slunk through an alley, and finally to the street which leads past the sugar refinery down to the power-house and the river. For many days after that I felt less envious of good old Haroun al Raschid.

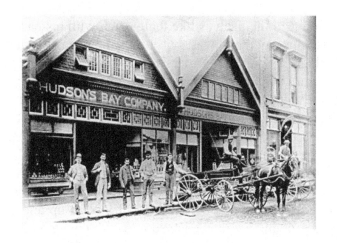

HBC store in Vancouver, c. 1890s

V - BILLINGS TO GLENDIVE

Getting round the power-dam did not prove a serious problem. The night man at the power-house told me it would be possible to land on the right side and let the boat down over a series of "steps" that had been built at that end of the dam. This was probably true, but as landing on the almost perpendicular cliff immediately above the drop-off looked a bit precarious I decided in favour of being safe by portaging rather than run the chance of being sorry through trying to line down. It was against just such emergencies as this that I had provided my feather-weight outfit.

A wooden skiff of the size of my steel one would have required at least four men to lift it up the forty-five degree slope of the bank above the intake of the power canal. It was not an easy task with my little shallop, but I managed it alone without undue exertion. Five minutes more sufficed to drag it a couple of hundred feet along the levee and launch it at the head of the rapid below the dam. Two trips brought down my outfit, and I was off into the river again.

Running at a slashing rate round the bend of the bluff, I kept on for a couple of miles or more to where the Northern Pacific and a highway bridge span the river a couple of miles from the centre of Billings. Leaving the boat and my outfit in the care of a genial pumping-house engineer, I phoned for a taxi and went up to the hotel behind closed curtains. To return to the scene of my last night's triumph as a mere river-rat and hack writer was a distinct anti-climax. As I had been warned by wire that a hundred pages of urgently needed proofs from New York would await me in Billings for correction, there was no side-stepping the necessity. The risk would have to be run, but to minimize it as far as was humanly possible I planned to keep to my room as much as I could, and to disguise myself by dressing as a gentleman or a drummer when I had to venture upon the streets. Then by keeping to the more refined parts of towns it seemed to me that I ought to stand a reasonably good chance of avoiding the poignancy of humiliation that would inevitably follow recognition by any of those fine fellows who had sat at my feet the night before. It was a well devised plan, and so came pretty near to succeeding.

I tumbled out of my bath into bed, stayed there an hour, got up, dressed in immaculate flannels and started in on the proofs. A reporter from the Gazette called up about noon to say he had been lying in ambush for me ever since the Livingston papers had warned him of my departure. Could he come over for a story? I couldn't very well refuse that, but took the precaution of throwing my "Indian Police" uniform in the closet before he arrived. Then I made a special point of telling him I always wore flannels and duck on my river trips—sort of survival of my South Sea yatching days. If he would only put that in, I reckoned, it would effectually drag a red herring across any suspicions that might be aroused by a reading of the story in the minds of my late subjects. He forgot it as a matter of fact, but it wasn't that that did the harm. It was just hard luck—Joss, as the sailors say.

The next day was the Fourth of July, a holiday, but a very obliging express agent, who came down town and opened up his office to let me get out a sleeping bag, made it unnecessary to hang on another night in Billings. The Gazette story brought no demonstrations—that is, of a hostile nature. Calls from scouting secretaries searching for a fatted calf to butcher for club holidays were the only ripples on the surface. Still with my fingers crossed, I ordered a closed taxi for the run down to my boat. It would have been a perfectly clean get-away had not Joss decreed that I should leave my package at the railway station to be picked up as I went by. Returning to the taxi from the check-room a man was waiting for me outside of the door.

"My name is Allstein," he began; but I had observed that before he opened his hard-set jaw. Without waiting for him to go on I made one wild, despairing bid to keep my honour white. I feel to this day that it deserved to have succeeded.

"Came in on the brake-beams, going out on shank's mare," I chirruped blithely, and forthwith (to the very evident perturbation of the taxi-driver) started as if off for Miles City on foot. Some will say my reasoning was quixotic, but this was the way of it at any rate: I cared no whit if hardware-drummer Allstein believed I was a hobo, just as long as he continued to believe I was an ex-sparring partner of Jack Dempsey. And what he must be prevented from knowing at any cost was that, far from being even the hammiest of ham-and-sparring partners, I was what the Gazette cub had characterized as a "daring novelist seeking material for new book by running rapids of Yellowstone."

But the fat was already in the fire. Allstein halted my Miles City Marathon with a gesture half weary, half contemptuous. "That taxi looks about as much like you're hoboing as did them three dishes of strawberries at the Northern this morning," he growled, glowering. I caved at once and meekly asked him to get in and come down to see my little steel boat. Lightest outfit that ever went down river.... Boat and all my stuff weighed less than I did myself....

I was in the taxi by that time. Allstein had continued to register "Betrayed! Betrayed!" but had not moved to cut off my retreat. That was something to be thankful for anyhow. Not knowing what else to say, I remarked to the driver that it must be getting along toward boat-time. And so away we went. Allstein's reproachful gaze bored into my back until we swung out of eye-range into the Custer Trail. I know that I shall be reminded of him every time I see a ruined maiden in the movies or at Drury Lane to the end of my days.

Billings is a fine modern city, which makes me regret all the more that most of my daylight impressions of it had to be gained by peeking under a taxicab curtain. It is by long odds the largest town on the Yellowstone; in fact, I saw no city comparable with it for size and vigour until at Sioux City I came to the first of the packing-house metropolises of the Missouri. Billings owed its first prosperity to cattle and sheep and its fine strategic situation for distribution. Pastoral industries cut less of a figure today, but the town has continued to gain ground as the principal distributing centre for western Montana. That, with agricultural and power development, has brought mills and factories, and the town now ranks high among the manufacturing centres of the Northwest. I shall live in hopes of going back some-day and seeing Billings properly—as a visiting Chamber of Commerce booster or a Rotary excursionist, or something equally sans reproche.

The point where the Northern Pacific Railway bridge crosses the Yellowstone below Billings is of considerable interest historically. It was here that Clark ferried Sergeant Pryor and his remaining pack animals across the river, preliminary to the overland journey that was to be attempted with the animals to the Mandan Villages. Here, also, is the point that is popularly credited with being the high-water mark of steamboat navigation on the Yellowstone. On June 6, 1875, Captain Grant Marsh in the Josephine, conducting a rough survey of the river under the direction of General J. W. Forsyth, reached a point which he estimated to be forty-six miles above Pompey's Pillar, 250 miles above Powder River and 483 miles above the mouth of the Yellowstone. Major Joseph Mills Hanson, in his "Conquest of the Missouri," stirringly describes the climax of this remarkable voyage.

After leaving Pompey's Pillar "the great river, though apparently undiminished in volume, grew more and more swift, constantly breaking into rapids through which it was necessary to warp and spar the boat, while numberless small islands split the channel into chutes, no one of which was large enough for easy navigation. At times it seemed that a smooth stretch of water had been reached, ... but invariably just beyond another rapid would be encountered.... Before nightfall a tremendous rapid was encountered, and though, after a hard struggle, it was successfully passed, so forbidding was its aspect and so savage the resistance it offered, that it was appreciatively named 'Hell Roaring Rapids.' At the head of it the boat lay up for the night, with a line stretched to the bank ahead to help her forward in the morning. But when dawn came, General Forsyth, seeing the nature of the river in front, ordered out a reconnoitring party who marched up the bank for several miles examining the channel. On their return they reported the whole river ahead so broken up by islands and with so powerful a current that it could not be navigated without constant resort to warping and sparring.... General Forsyth and Captain Marsh held a consultation and decided that no adequate reward for the labour involved could be gained by going further. So, at two o'clock p. m. on June 7th, the boat was turned about and started on her return.... Before leaving this highest point attained, Captain Marsh blazed the trunk of a gigantic cottonwood to which the Josephine was tied, and carved thereon the name of the boat and the date. It is exceedingly improbable that a steam vessel will ever again come within sight of that spot or be entitled to place her name beneath the Josephine's on that ancient tree trunk, almost under the shadow of the Rocky Mountains."

The Josephine's farthest west on the Yellowstone stands as the record for steamers by many miles, but what wouldn't I have given to have found that big cottonwood and tied up there myself! No one along the river could tell me anything about it, and there is little doubt that, like so many thousands of its less distinguished brethren, it has been swallowed up by the spring floods. Neither above nor below the bridge for many miles, however, could I locate a riffle sufficiently savage to fit Captain Marsh's description of "Hell Roaring Rapids." It has occurred to me as just possible that such a rapid was wiped out when the power dam was built, the comparatively short distance the water is backed up at that point suggesting that the original fall was very considerable. Again, it is possible that to Captain Marsh, after his many years in the comparatively smooth waters of the Missouri, such riffles as still go slap-banging down along the bluffs opposite Billings would appear a lot rougher than they would to one just down from the almost continuously white and rock-torn rapids of the upper river.

At any event it stirred my imagination mightily to locate the Josephine's turning point even approximately. From now on I was going to have a fellow pilot for Captain Clark. Captain Grant Marsh was henceforth at my call at any point I needed him between Billings and St. Louis. The stout frame of that splendid old river Viking had been tucked under the sod down Bismarck-way for a number of years, but I knew his spirit still took its wonted tricks at the wheel. Captain William Clark and Captain Grant Marsh! Could you beat that pair if it came to standing watch-and-watch down the Yellowstone and Missouri? And there were others waiting just round the bend. At the Big Horn I could sign on Manual Lisa if I wanted him; or John Colter, who discovered the Yellowstone Park while flying from the Blackfeet. But Colter was not truthful, which disqualified him for pilotage. I should have to ship him simply as a congenial spirit—one of my own kind.

Returning to my boat, I found that the little daughters of the pumping-station man had roofed it over like a Venetian gondola and moved in with all their worldly goods. They confronted me with the clean-cut alternatives of coming to live with them right there or taking them with me down the river. Fortunately their parents intervened on my side. With the aid of those two kindly and tactful diplomats—and a lot of milk chocolate and dried apricots—I finally contrived an ejection. The operation delayed me till after four o'clock, though, so there was no hope of making Pompey's Pillar that night.

Though I knew that the fall of the river would be easing off very rapidly from now on, there was little indication of it in the twenty-five-mile stretch I ran before dark that evening. Bouncing back and forth between broken lines of red-yellow bluffs, there were frequent sharp riffles and even two or three corners where considerable water was splashed in. For only the shortest of reaches was the stream sufficiently quiet to allow me to take my eyes off it long enough to enjoy the really entrancing diorama of the scenery. I was especially sorry for this, for on my right was unfolding the verdant loveliness of the Crow Reservation, the very heart of the hunting grounds which the Indians had loved above all others for hundreds of years—the region they had fought hardest to save from relinquishment to the relentless white. Read what, according to Irving in the "Adventures of Captain Bonneville," an Absaroka said about this Red Man's Garden of Eden a hundred years ago:

"The Crow country is a good country. The Great Spirit has put it in exactly the right place; while you are in it you fare well; whenever you go out of it, whichever way you travel, you fare worse." After going on to tell of the unspeakable climatic conditions and the scarcity of game prevailing in the regions to the north, south, east and west, this progenitor of the modern booster goes on: "The Crow country is in exactly the right place. It has snowy mountains and sunny plains; all kinds of climate and good things for every season. When summer heats scorch the prairies, you can draw up under the mountains where the air is sweet and cool, the grass fresh, and the bright streams come tumbling out of the snowy-banks. There you can hunt the elk, the deer and the antelope, when their skins are fit for dressing; there you will find plenty of white bears and the mountain sheep.

"In the autumn, when your horses are fat and strong from the mountain pastures, you can go down to the plains and hunt buffalo, or trap beaver on the streams. And when winter comes, you can take shelter in the woody bottoms along the rivers; there you will find buffalo meat for yourselves and cottonwood bark for your horses; or you may winter in the Wind River valley, where there is salt weed in abundance.

"The Crow country is exactly in the right place. Everything good is to be found there. There is no country like the Crow country."

Like the scent of fern leaves wafted out of the dear, dead past, those lines awakened in my heart memories of something that had long gone out of my life.

"Something is, or something seems,
Which touches me with mystic gleams,
Like glimpses of forgotten dreams ...
Of something seen, I know not where,
Such as no language may declare."

I muttered that in fragments, but the lines only adumbrated the longing without revealing its hidden fount. Still groping mentally, I unwrapped some forks and spoons done up in a page of the Los Angeles Times. Ah, that gave me the cue! Los Angeles Chamber of Commerce tourist literature. And to think a Crow Indian started that kind of a thing!

Running until the river bottoms were swamped in purple shadows, I landed and made camp in a soft little nest of snowy sand left behind by a high-water eddy. There was an abrupt yellow cliff rising straight out of a woolly-white riffle on the right bank, and beyond a grove of cottonwood to the left were the shadowy buildings of some kind of a ranch. Even in the deepening twilight I could read something of the record of its growth—groups of log cabins, groups of unpainted, roughsawed lumber and finally a huge red barn and a great square, verandahed house that was all but a mansion. I was wondering if the same pioneering frontiersman who had built the cabins had survived to occupy the big green and white house, when the soft southerly wind brought the scent of sweet clover and the strains of a phonograph. "Evening Star," the Jocelyn Lullaby, the Baccarole, wafted me their "convoluted runes" one after the other; then a piano began to strum and a girl, neither mean of voice nor temperament, sang Tosti's "Good-Bye." It always had had a softly sentimentalizing effect on me, that "Lines of white on a sullen Sea," sung (as it always is) the night before the steamer reaches port. And here it was getting me in the same old place—that mushy spot under the solar plexus that non-anatomically trained poets confuse with the heart. I simply had to hike over and tell that impassioned songstress how perfectly her song matched the scent of sweet clover. Cleaning up the last of the dried apricot stew in my army mess tin, I pushed southward across the moonlit bar. No luck. I was on an island.

I tried out my new bed for the first time that night. It turned out to be a combination of a canvas bag and inflatable rubber mattress, called by its makers a "Sleeping Pocket." Here again it transpired I had played in luck in the matter of a pig bought in a poke. I used that precious little ten-pound packet of rubber and canvas all the way to New Orleans without blankets. On wind-blown sand bars, mud-banks, coal barges or the greasy steel decks of engine-rooms it was ever the same—always dry, always soft, always warm. Comfortable sleeping measures just about the whole difference between the success and failure of many a trip. I shudder to think of the messy nights I must inevitably have suffered had all those lurking thunder-storms that I weathered so snugly caught me in blankets.

I overslept the next morning and so did not carry out my over-night resolution of pulling across to the ranch and thanking the "Good-Bye" girl. Or rather, I did start and then changed my mind. She was on the upper verandah recuperating from a shampoo. Scarlet kimono and bobbed hair! No, not with a river to escape by. Stifling my au revoir impulse I decided to leave well enough alone by taking that "Good-bye" literally. Abandoning the boat to the will of the current I departed via the lines of white under the sullen cliff.

At the end of a couple of hours' run in a slackening current I landed in an eddy above Pompey's Pillar, quite the most outstanding landmark on the Yellowstone. Clark describes how he halted "to examine a very remarkable rock situated in an extensive bottom on the right, about two hundred and fifty paces from the shore. It is nearly four hundred paces in circumference, two hundred feet high and accessible from the northeast, the other sides being a perpendicular cliff of a light-coloured, gritty rock.... The Indians have carved the figures of animals and other objects on the sides of the rock, and on the top are raised two piles of stones." Captain Clark, after writing down a careful description of the country on all sides, marked his name and the date on the rock and went on his way.

This was the first point at which I had opportunity to make accurate comparison of the respective stages of water encountered by Clark and myself. I found the base of the rock less than a hundred paces from the river, which indicated—as the channel seems to have been well fixed here—that I was enjoying three or four feet more water than did my illustrious predecessor. This would seem to be just about accounted for by the fact that I was voyaging three weeks earlier in the season than he—that much nearer the high water of early June, at which time it was apparent that the river backed up right to the cliff.

Add the telegraph poles of a distant railway line and a picnic booth littered with papers and watermelon rinds, and Clark's description of what was unrolled to him from the top of Pompey's Pillar would stand today. I located the place where his name had been carved by a grating which the Northern Pacific engineers had erected to protect it from vandals, but the most careful scrutiny failed to reveal any trace of the letters themselves. The practical obliteration of what is probably the only authentic physical mark of their passing that either Lewis or Clark left between St. Louis and the mouth of the Columbia is hardly compensated for by the presence of several hundred somewhat later and rather less important signatures at this point. Several of these latter bore the date of the previous day—July 4th, 1921,—and so represented a bold bid for fame on the part of some of the watermelon guzzling picnickers. One of these had even pried a bar aside in a not entirely successful endeavour to emblazon his name in the protected area. It was all rather annoying. These new names are piling up very fast with the coming of the flivver, but it is going to take a lot of them to make up for the one they have blotted out.

Clark's apparent mental processes in the christening of Pompey's Pillar are rather amusing. Neither a profound historian nor a classicist, the Captain still had a sort of vague idea in his head that there was some kind of a rocky erection out Nile-way named after Pompey. That being so, what could be more fitting—since the names of all of the members of his own party had been used a half dozen times over first and last—than that this rocky eminence by the Yellowstone should be called after Pompey. That he was not clear in his mind as to the character of the historic original at Alexandria is evidenced by the fact that he first called the Yellowstone prototype "Pompy's Tower." Whether he or his publisher was responsible for the subsequent change to "Pillar" is not clear. As a matter of fact the latter is only a detached fragment of "the high romantic clifts" that Clark observed jutting over the water on the opposite side of the river. It bears about as much actual resemblance to the real Pompey's Pillar as the Enchanted Mesa does to Cleopatra's Needle.

The river was broader and slower below Pompey's Pillar, with the rapids shorter and farther between. At five I landed at a very pretty alfalfa ranch on the left bank to inquire about passing what appeared to be a submerged dam some hundreds of yards ahead. Only two women were at home—a beaming old lady and her very stout daughter. They insisted on my staying to tea, which required no great persuasiveness on their part after Joanna remarked that she was out of breath from turning the ice-cream freezer. The girl was astonishingly red, round and sweet—a veritable bifurcated apple. She seemed to have a very good knowledge of the river, and assured me I should have no trouble at the diversion dam provided I kept well toward the left bank. Indeed, if I thought it would help at all, she would ride down with me and show the way. There was a path back home from their lower pasture.

Considering how shy I had found most of the rancher folk to be of the river, this game offer pretty nearly took my breath away. I would have been all for accepting it save for one very good and sufficient reason—it was physically impossible. I had noticed that Joanna's personal chair was of home construction, and considerable amplitude of beam—certainly six inches more than the stern-sheets of my slender shallop. She could wedge in sidewise, of course, but that still left the matter of a life-preserver. I didn't feel it was quite the thing to take an only child into a rapid without some provision for floating her out in case of an upset. And my Gieve wouldn't do. The inflated "doughnut" that slipped so easily up and down my own brawny brisket would just about have served Joanna as an armlet. So I declined with what grace I could, and we all parted on the best of terms—I with a fragrant flitch of their home-cured bacon, they with three double handfuls of my California home-dried apricots.

I had no trouble at the dam, which was only on the right side, where it had been erected to divert the water into the head of an irrigation ditch. Running until nearly dark, I landed and made camp on a breeze-swept bar away from the mosquitos.

I passed the mouth of the Big Horn in mid-forenoon of the following day. I should have liked to land but was fearful I would get out of hand and take too much time once I turned myself loose at the one point above all others where the most Yellowstone history has been made. The Big Horn was known in a vague way through the Indian accounts of it even before the time of Lewis and Clark, but the first permanent establishment upon it was the trading post which Manuel Lisa erected there in 1807. It was to this point that John Colter fled after being chased by the Blackfeet across Yellowstone Park, and it was his point of departure in a canoe on a voyage to St. Louis which he claimed to have made in thirty days. Colter's account of how he ran down several black-tail deer and bighorn before relaxing the tremendous burst of speed he had put on to distance the Redskins never bothered me much, but that average of close to a hundred miles a day—most of it down the languid Missouri—somehow won't stick. I found I couldn't keep it up even after I put on my engine. Colter undoubtedly exaggerated about his time on this trip, and that being true, doubtless, also, about trampling underfoot the deer and bighorn. Colter was a liar but not an artistic one. Now if old Jim Bridger had been telling that canoe-voyage yarn he would doubtless have hung a bag of alum over the bow and shrunk the distance as a starter, and then probably used a trained catfish for auxiliary power. That's the kind of liar that makes the world safe for democracy.

Post after post was founded at the confluence of the Yellowstone and Big Horn until, in the 'seventies, it became the centre of operations for the Army in the greatest of our Indian wars. In comparison with the broad, rolling tide of the Yellowstone the turbid current of the tributary appeared shallow and of no great volume—the last place in the world for a river steamer to venture with any hope of going its own length without grounding. And yet, I reflected, the Big Horn could have been scarcely higher on that sultry Sunday of June 25th, 1876, when Captain Grant Marsh, acting on orders from General Terry, sparred and warped and crabbed the wonderful old Far West up twenty-five miles of those rock-choked, foam-white rapids. The skies to the south were black with rolling smoke clouds, but with nothing to indicate that under their shadows five companies of the 7th Cavalry were paying with their lives for the precipitancy of their brave but hot-headed commander. The next day the Far West reached, passed and returned to the mouth of the Little Big Horn, and it was there that a half-crazed Crow scout, all but speechless with terror, brought on the first lap of its way to the outer world the story of the Custer Massacre.

On the morning of June 30th, with Major Reno's wounded aboard, the Far West cast off for the start of her epic run to Fort Lincoln. Major Joseph Hanson records that that Captain Marsh all but collapsed in the pilot-house as the terrible responsibility of that fifty-three-mile run

131

down the rock-paved channel of the Big Horn suddenly assailed him on stepping to the wheel. General Terry had just said to him: "Captain, you have on board the most precious cargo a boat ever carried. Every soldier here who is suffering with wounds is the victim of a terrible blunder; a sad and terrible blunder." Crabbing up stream with supplies was one thing, floundering down with a shattered human cargo of that kind, quite another. Captain Marsh declared the moment the most sickening of his life. Then he pulled himself together and drove her through. I tried to imagine the relief her skipper must have felt as he rounded that last bend above where I now saw a railway bridge and headed the Far West into the deep, clear channel of the Yellowstone, but couldn't come near to compassing it. A man has to have carried a load of that kind to know what it means to put it down. The Far West broke all upper river records for speed in her run to Fort Lincoln, below Bismarck, the nearest hospital. Captain Marsh's splendid achievement in saving Reno's wounded by his masterly navigation is the one bright bit of silver lining on the sodden black cloud of the Massacre of the Little Big Horn.

At the mouth of the Rosebud I passed another important rendezvous of the Sioux campaign. From here, after taking his final orders from General Terry, Custer had departed on the march that was to finish upon the Little Big Horn. Major Hanson relates an incident that occurred here an hour or two after the ill-fated command had disappeared up the valley, and which was particularly interesting to me at the moment as it involved the upset of a skiff in a riffle I was about to run. All of the letters written by Custer's men since leaving Fort Lincoln were put in a bag and started by boat for Fort Buford. "Sergeant Fox and two privates of the escort were detailed to carry the precious cargo down," wrote Major Hanson. "Amid a chorus of hearty cheers from the people on the steamer, they started out. But they were totally unfamiliar with the handling of a small boat in the swirling current of the Yellowstone. Before they had gone fifty feet their skiff overturned. There, in full view of all their comrades, who could not reach them in time to save, all three of the unfortunate fellows sank from sight, while the mail sack went to the bottom of the river."

The soldiers were drowned, but persistent dragging of the river under the direction of Captain Marsh finally brought up the mail sack, thus saving for their relatives and friends the last letters of the men who were to fall before the Sioux a few days later. These included Custer's note to his wife as well as young Boston Custer's letter to his mother. Sending three inexperienced soldiers to boat down the Yellowstone with so humanly precious a freight in their care cannot but strike one as about on all fours with other blunders that led up to the tragic climax of that disastrous campaign.

I found a shallow bar clawed with sprawling channels but no riffles to speak of below the Rosebud. There could hardly have been bad water there at any time.

Landing at a grassy point to make camp about seven-thirty I found the mosquitos so thick that I beat a hasty retreat to the boat and pushed off again in search of a gravel bar in midstream. The sight of new and comfortable ranch buildings lured me to land a half mile below, however, where an invitation to spend the night in the screened bunk-house was promptly forthcoming. The ranch turned out to be a part of an extensive irrigation enterprise, promoted and managed by a chap named Cummings from Minneapolis, who chanced to be on the place at the time. Except for the general farming depression, prospects were good, he said—better than in the dry farming sections, where crops, already very short, were being still further shortened by grasshoppers. He was rather more optimistic than the run of Montanan pastoralists and agriculturalists I had met, all of whom had been having terribly hard sledding.

A leisurely three-hour's run in the morning brought me to Fort Keogh and Miles City, respectively above and below the Tongue. The red-brown current of the latter tinged the Yellowstone for a mile below their confluence. Clark camped at the mouth of the Tongue, and his painstaking description of the second in size of the Yellowstone's tributaries might have been written today.

"It has a very wide bed.... The water is of a light-brown colour and nearly milk-warm; it is shallow and its rapid current throws out great quantities of mud and some coarse gravel.... The warmth of the water would seem to indicate that the country through which it passes is open and without shade."

Captain Clark was a splendid geographer, even if he did run amuck a bit with his historical nomenclature.

The annual Round-up had come to an end the previous day, so that I found Miles City, if not quite a banquet hall deserted, at least in something of a morning-after frame of mind. It rather warmed one's heart to see so many people rubbing throbbing temples, and I seemed to see in it some explanation of what a cowboy meant when he told me that the only critter at the Round-up that he couldn't ride was the "White Mule."

All the cities of the Yellowstone have character and individuality, and none more than Miles City. Not so beautifully located as Livingston, not quite so metropolitan as Billings, there is something in the fine, broad streets of Miles that suggests the frank, bluff, open-heartedness of a cowboy straight from the ranges. The town looks you squarely between the eyes and says "Put it there"! in a deep, mellow voice that goes straight to the heart. That voice and that look embody the quintessence of reassurance. You know in an instant that you are face to face with the kind of a town that couldn't play a mean trick on a man if it tried—that there isn't going to be any need of slinking around with one hand on your wallet and the other on your hip-pocket. Even though you may have been warned that various sorts of rough stuff have been pulled in Miles, you are certain that outsiders will have been found at the bottom of it if all the facts were known. (My over-night stop in Miles was hardly sufficient to prove out the truth of all this. Just the same, that's the way I felt about the town, and that's the way I still feel.)

Miles City owed its early importance to sheep and cattle, and still has the distinction of being the principle horse market of America. Agriculture has played an increasingly important part in its later growth. The splendid valleys of the Powder and the Tongue are both tributary territory, while the irrigation of the rich lands of the Yellowstone is bringing year by year an augmented flow of wealth to the city's gates. (Darn it! I wonder if I have cribbed that last sentence from Chamber of Commerce literature. In any event, it is quite true in this case.)

Besides its extensive cattle and sheep ranges, the Miles City region distinguishes itself by having the greatest range of temperature of any place in the world. The Government Weather Bureau is authority for the fact that a winter temperature of sixty-five degrees below Zero has been balanced by a summer one of one hundred and fifteen above. Neither California nor the Riviera can give the tourist anything like that variety to choose from. From Esquimo to Hottentot, what race couldn't establish itself right there by the Yellowstone under almost normal home weather conditions? Of course, if they were going to establish themselves for long some kind of a meteorological Joshua would be needed to command the thermometer to stand still; also some one to see that the command was carried out. And there would lie the way to complications and friction, for one can hardly imagine a Hottentot Joshua quite in agreement with an Esquimo Joshua as to just what point the thermometer should be commanded to stand at. That might be solved by the establishment of thermostat villages, but then would arise the endless train of legal complications inevitably following in the wake of infringing on the riparian rights (whatever they are) of the irrigation people. No, probably Miles had best be left to its present inhabitants, who appear to have waxed both amiable and prosperous by browsing on their temperature ranges just as Nature provided them.

I made special inquiry about Buffalo Rapids while in Miles City. This was for two reasons. Reading that Clark had been compelled to let down his boats over an abrupt fall of several feet at that point, I thought it just as well not to go blundering into it myself without further information. I also heard that there was a project for developing extensive power at this series of riffles. I spent a pleasant and profitable afternoon with Mr. Doane, the engineer of the project. He said that I ought to have little trouble in running right through all of the rapids, but suggested it might be well to land at a farmhouse near the head and see for myself. He also gave me a few facts about the power project. I would have to refer to my notes (which I never do if at all avoidable) to recall the hydro-electric data; but I need no such adventitious aid to remember Mrs. Doane's freshly distilled "Essence of Dandelion." Literal liquid golden sunshine it was, with a bouquet recalling to me that of an ambrosial decoction made by the monks of Mount Athos from buds of asphodel, and which a masked hermit lets down to you on a string from the tower in which he is supposed to be walled up with the makings and his retorts. Buffalo Rapids never troubled me again.

I pushed off about eleven in the forenoon of July 8th, and an hour's run in moderately fast water took me within sight and sound of the white caps of the first pitch of Buffalo Rapids. Clark had originally named these riffles "Buffaloe Shoal, from the circumstance of one of these animals being found in them." He describes it further as a "succession of bad shoals, interspersed with hard, brown, gritty rock, extending for six miles; the last shoal stretches nearly across the river, and has a descent of about three feet. At this place we were obliged to let the canoes down by hand, for fear of their splitting on a concealed rock; though when the shoals are known a large canoe could pass with safety through the worst of them. This is the most difficult part of the whole Yellowstone River...."

Captain Clark would hardly have registered the latter verdict had he run the Yellowstone all the way from the Big Bend, where he first came upon it. Indeed, it seems to me that he must have run rapids above Billings that were quite as menacing as the one which now put his party to so much trouble to avoid. I would not be too dogmatic on that point, however. A hundred years of time bring great changes even to bedrock riffles, and these latter themselves also vary greatly according to the stage of water. I was assured that from August on there is still a nearly abrupt drop of several feet at one point in Buffalo Rapids.

Although I was sure I could see my way past the first riffle without serious difficulty, I still thought it best to learn what I could at the farm-house Doane had indicated. This proved to be a comfortable old log structure at a point where the right bank was being rapidly torn down by the swift current. A very deaf chap at the first door I approached strongly urged that I line all the way down, saying that there was at least one point where my boat could not possibly live. As that wasn't quite what I wanted to hear, I went round the house and tried another door. Here, in a big, fragrant kitchen, I found a family at lunch, but with one nice, juicy helping of cream-splashed tapioca pudding still uncon-sumed. I helped them out with that, and in return asked for information about the rapids. None of them was river-broke, but they said they had seen a rowboat run down the left side of the first riffle the previous summer and that they afterwards heard it was not upset until it got to Wolf Rapids, down Terry-way. That was more encouraging, at least as far as Buffalo Rapids were concerned, and I decided to push off and let Nature take its course. All of them, including the careful deaf brother, came down to speed me on. Rather anxious for a bit more weight aft to bring the head higher, I asked if any of them cared to run through with me to the railway bridge below the bend. All of them shook their heads save a flower-like slip of a girl of fourteen or thereabouts. She would have been game, I think—had the proper encouragement from her mother been forthcoming. What a handicap a solicitous mother is to a flower-like child! This mother was rather an old dear, too. All I really held against her at the last was on the score of letting her emergency reserve of tapioca and cream sink so low.

The way past the worst of the first riffle looked so clear on the right that I did not trouble to pull across to the other side. I ran through in easy, undulant water, without being forced uncomfortably close to some patches of rather savage looking white where the teeth of the bed-rock were flecked with tossing foam. Rounding a wide bend, I found myself drifting down onto the main run of riffles, the passing of one of which caused Clark's party some trouble. These filled the channel much more completely than did those above, and it hardly looked possible to avoid bad water all of the way through. Even so, there was nothing that looked wicked enough to be worth landing to avoid.

Pulling hard to the right, I gave good berth to a line of badly messed up combers with not enough foam on them to cover all of the black-rock ledge beneath. Then, feeling more or less on easy street, I let the skiff slowly draw in toward the middle of a long, straight line of smoothly-running rollers that extended to and under the long railway bridge. I could have kept clear of the worst of this water by hard work, but with the beautifully rounded waves signalling "All clear"! as far as snags and really hostile rocks were concerned it seemed too bad to miss the fun. Wallowing somewhat wildly now and then and shipping a good bit of water in her dives, my little tin shallop went through like a duck. I knew I was getting down toward the end of that kind of thrills and it was well to make hay while the sun shone.

Before I was out of the rapid a long overland rolled out upon and over the bridge below. The engine gave me a friendly toot and waving hands down the winding line of coaches gave the train the look of a giant centipede trying to pirouette with all of its port-side legs. Warned by what had happened to me under similar circumstances in the riffle under Rapids Station, I kept my eye right on the ball to the end of the swing. A few days later, in the hotel at Glendive, a notions drummer told me he had been on the observation platform on the occasion in question, adding jocularly that every one there had been wishing I would pull a spill for them. "Cose why?" I asked him just a bit bluntly; "those rapids have been known to drown a buffalo."

Perhaps I should not have been quite so abrupt, for that was what cramped the delightfully drummeresque ingenuousness with which he had begun. Muttering something about "breaking the monotony of a run through the Bad Lands," the good chap backed off and out of my life. I was sorry for that, sorry to have embarrassed him, and especially sorry I didn't have the savoir faire to make it easy for him to finish as frankly as he opened up. I didn't blame him and his friends for wishing for that spill. I know perfectly well I would have hoped for it myself had our positions been reversed. Almost any good red-blooded human would get a kick out of watching, from a nice, dry car platform, another good red-blooded human bumping-the-bumps down a rocky riffle. But I would never have been honest enough to confess my hopes—to the man who might have figured in the spill, that is. That was where this chap with the notions line would always have me one down. And what a shame it was I couldn't hold him long enough to learn how he made himself that way.

"Buffaloe Shoal" was the first of what one might call Clark's "Menagerie Series" of rapids. The next, twenty miles below, was named Bear Rapid, because they saw a bear standing there. The third, two miles below the mouth of the Powder, was christened Wolf Rapid, "from seeing a wolf there." Clark describes Bear Rapids as "a shoal, caused by a number of rocks strewed over the river; but though the waves are high, there is a very good channel to the left, which renders the passage secure." Wolf is dismissed as "a rapid of no great danger." A hundred spring floods have doubtless had the effect of worsening Wolf—a bedrock rapid—somewhat, and of scouring out the worst of the boulders in Bear. I found the latter only an inconsiderable riffle, but the Wolf still showed some mighty vicious fangs. They were easy enough to avoid in a light skiff, but the old steamboat skippers always reckoned there was more potential trouble lying in ambush in the cracks of these shallowly submerged reefs of black rock than at any other place on the navigated Yellowstone or Missouri.

The Powder is the last of the great southerly tributaries of the Yellowstone. Sprawling over a shifting estuary in several runlets, it looked much as it must have appeared to Clark when he wrote: "The water is very muddy, and like its banks of a dark brown colour. Its current throws out great quantities of red stones; which circumstances, with the appearance of the distant hills, induced Captain Clark to call it the Red-stone, which he afterward found to be the meaning of its Indian name, Wahasah." At his camp here Clark found the buffalo prowling so close during the night that "they excited much alarm, lest in crossing the river they should tread on the boats and split them to pieces."

Below the Powder the river flows for some distance through an extensive belt of Bad Lands, a burnt, barren, savage-looking country with little vegetation, few streams, and miles of fantastic castles, kiosks and minarets of black and red rock. It is desolate in the extreme even when viewed from the cool current of the river, but surely in no wise so sinister and forbidding as those terrible stretches of Bad Lands be-tween the Yellowstone and Little Missouri which grim old General Sully, after pursuing the Sioux over their scorched rocks for a season, so aptly described as "Hell-With-the-Lights-Out."

Finding Terry was out of sight behind the hills, I landed about eight o'clock to make camp on a gravel bar. A grizzled old codger, across whose fish-lines I came crabbing in, seemed more pleased than put out over the diversion. He could fish twenty-four hours a day, he explained, but a man willing to be talked to wasn't the sort of a bird that came along to that neck of the river every day. So he went up to his cabin, brought down some eggs and milk, and we pooled grub and suppered together there under the cottonwoods by the river. He had hunted, trapped, prospected and searched for agates for fifty years, and it was well into the night before he had told me all about it. A confession of my old love for "Calamity Jane" broke down his reserve at the outset. He had seen a lot of the dear old girl at the very zenith of her career. He told a delicious story of how "Calamity," her paprika temperament ruffled by a dude's red necktie, had tried to make that unfortunate eat the offending rag at the point of a pistol. The advice with which she had endeavoured to sauce the untoothsome morsel was rather the best part of the yarn, but it was hardly sufficiently "drawing-room" to find place in these chaste chronicles.

There was a strong up-river breeze blowing when I got under way at six the next morning. When this came dead ahead it had no effect other than slowing down my progress greatly, but when the direction of the channel brought it more or less abeam I had great difficulty in keeping from being blown under the caving banks. This was, as I re-member it, my first experience of what later became perhaps the most annoyingly persistent difficulty attending my progress down both the Missouri and Mississippi. After getting in trouble two or three times and having to stop to bail out and recover my wind, I gave up the fight about noon and landed at a highly picturesque old ranch twenty-five miles above Glendive. The clanging of a dinner gong was not the least pleasant sound that assailed my ears as I climbed the bank.

Belonging to Charley Krug of Glendive, the place was one of the oldest and most historic of Montana cattle ranches. Built in the Indian days, and in an extremely windy section of country, the buildings appeared to be something of a compromise between forts and cyclone cellars. Nothing short of a "Big Bertha" could have made much impression upon the enormous cottonwood logs—and the Sioux, I believe, had nothing heavier than Springfields.

The professional personnel of the outfit was wrapped in gloom over the advent of a devastating light of grasshoppers that was rapidly cleaning up the ranges down to the gravel. This sodden shroud, however, did not blanket the cook—an exception of importance from my standpoint. This individual was a part-time wrestler and prize-fighter, abandoning the squared-circle for the pots and pans only in the off seasons. He introduced himself to me as "Happy" Coogan, and then proceeded to show why he was so called. Backing me up behind a food barrage, he sang a song, danced a jig, illustrated Jack Dempsey's left hook and Gotch's "toe-hold" on a half-breed cow-puncher, and then challenged all-comers at a "catch-as-catch-can" rough-and-tumble with nothing barred but gouging and biting. Now who could worry about grasshoppers with a man like that around?

"Happy" recited excerpts from his ring career all afternoon while I ate apple pie with cream poured over it and waited for the wind to cease. It was falling lighter by five, but my host would not hear of my leaving before supper. Impromptu cabaret work lengthened that banquet out to eight o'clock, and it was early twilight before I finally broke away and went down to push off. "Happy" followed me down, his arms filled with eggs, milk, jams, pies and various other comestibles. "Don't like to let a man go off hungry," he explained. "Never know when I may be needing a hand-out myself."

Bless your generous heart, "Happy"; I only hope I may be cruising in your vicinity if you ever need that hand-out. That bucket of

California home-dried apricots I left you didn't go toward balancing our grub account.

With no very swift water ahead and the prospect of a fairly clear night, I had hopes for a while of drifting right on through to Glendive. These hopes—along with me and my outfit—were dampened by a shower shortly after I started, and completely dashed by a steady drizzle that set in about nine. Dragging up the skiff on the first bar on which it grounded in the now pitchy darkness, I inflated my sleeping-pocket, crawled into it and went to sleep. Awakening at dawn to find a cloudless sky, I crawled out, pushed off, and was in Glendive before six o'clock. Landing half a mile above town, I climbed up to a shack which "Happy" Coogan had told me was owned by a friend of his who had worked in the local pool-room. It was no sort of hour to awaken a tired business man of a Sunday morning, but "Happy's" name proved open sesame. It took some rearranging to get my stuff into that ten-by-twelve shack with a man, his wife and their seven children. Somehow we managed it, however; moreover, the whole nine of them pledged themselves to stand watch-and-watch over the skiff until I showed up again, no matter how long that might be. The true river spirit had awakened even in these dwellers on the fringes of Glendive's municipal dump. Bath, breakfast, snooze and another séance with inevitable proofs was the order of the day.

Poster for 1912 film The Life of Buffalo Bill

In Gardner Canon

Gardner River Crossing, 1901

VI - GLENDIVE TO THE MISSOURI

Glendive, located on the Yellowstone at a point where the Northern Pacific leaves the river to cut across the Bad Lands straight for the plains of North Dakota, owes more to the railroad than perhaps any other town of the valley. Although Glendive Creek was a frequent halt in the steamboat days of the Indian campaigns, there was never much of a settlement there until railway construction commenced in the late 'seventies. The first train pulled into Glendive almost forty years to a day previous to my arrival by boat. I found a fine, clean, prosperous little city of 6000 where my puffing predecessor had drawn up to little more than a typical frontier construction camp. Range stock helped the town along in its earlier days, but the railway shops probably did more. Finally the completion of the dam at Intake and the distribution of water to the most extensive irrigable area in the Yellowstone Valley provided a tributary agricultural territory of great wealth.

There was one thing I was especially interested in seeing in Glendive—a school musical system that is probably without a near rival in any town in America five times as large. I was assured that, of a school enrolment of about a thousand, nearly two hundred pupils played some kind of a musical instrument. There was an orchestra of sixty pieces, and a boy's military band of sixty-five. Each was divided into junior and senior grades, and a member was pushed ahead or dropped back according to talent and effort. At no time did a pupil have a place cinched; nothing but steady conscientious effort, regular attendance at rehearsals, and proper general deportment won promotion, or prevented demotion. Perhaps the finest thing about the whole system, was the fact that it was undertaken entirely apart from the regular curriculum, no school credits whatever being given for the work. I was told the credit for this fine achievement belonged to a principal of one of the grade schools, a Miss Lucille Hennigar, who had put herself behind it purely out of love of music and children.

I did not have the honour of meeting Miss Hennigar, but I did make the acquaintance of some of her protégés. First and last, about two score of them must have chanced along in the hour I was tinkering with my boat late Sunday afternoon. They were regular fellows all right (every other one wanted to come down in the morning and sign on with me), but not a hoodlum in the lot. Not a mother's darling of them tried to kick a hole in my little tin shallop. As none of them exhibited any symptoms of infantile paralysis, I decided it must be music—quieting the mean foot as well as soothing the savage breast.

Warned by every authority from Captain Clark to an agate-hunter I had passed at the mouth of the Powder that I was now approaching the "Mosquito Coast" of the Yellowstone, I made special point of preparing to go into battle by getting the best kind of a sleep I could in Glendive. This made it particularly gratifying to find that this good little city had just about the cleanest, most comfortable and best run hotel in the valley. I should have paid it that tribute even had not its genial manager, in company with the Secretary of the Chamber of Commerce, driven down to see me off—bringing an especially appealing little cold lunch.

It was late in the forenoon before I got away. Just as I was about to push off a telegram was brought down to me from Mr. A. M. Cleland, Passenger Traffic Manager of the Northern Pacific, saying that he had heard of my trip and was wiring all the company's agents along the river to be on the watch to lend me a hand, and to consider any of the N. P.'s shops at my service for repairs. Even though it arrived at the very moment I was turning away from the main line of the Northern Pacific, which I had paralleled all the way from Livingston, I was nevertheless just as appreciative of the spirit that prompted the courteous and kindly message.

Captain Clark had made camp just above Glendive,[1] "where they saw the largest white bear that any of the party had ever before seen, devouring a dead buffalo on a sand bar. They fired two balls into him; he then swam to the mainland and walked along the shore. Captain Clark pursued him and lodged two more balls in his body; but though he bled profusely he made his escape, as night prevented them from following him."

As the country below Glendive is probably both the richest and most intensively cultivated in the whole Yellowstone Valley, I was especially struck by the contrast presented by verdant irrigated fields of alfalfa and clover to the howling wilderness Clark described. Nowhere else in all of his journey back and forth across the continent had he seen such a variety and such numbers of animals. It must have been somewhere below the present site of the great Government dam at Intake that the buffalo began to appear in vast numbers. As their boat floated down "a herd happened to be on their way across the river. Such was the multitude of these animals that, though the river, including an island over which they passed, was a mile wide, the herd stretched, as thickly as they could swim, from one side to the other, and the party was obliged to stop for an hour." Forty-five miles below, two other herds as numerous as the first blocked their way again.

The following day they found the "buffalo and elk, as well as the pursuers of both, the wolves, in great numbers." Moreover, "the bears, which gave so much trouble on the head of the Missouri, are equally fierce in this quarter. This morning one of them, which was on a sand-bar as the boat passed, raised himself on his hind legs; and after looking at the party, plunged in and swam toward them. He was received with three balls in the body; he then turned around and made for the shore. Toward evening another entered the water to swim across. Captain Clark ordered the boat toward the shore, and just as the bear landed, shot the animal in the head. It proved to be the largest female they had ever seen, so old that its tusks were worn quite smooth. The boats escaped with difficulty between two herds of buffalo that were crossing the river." On this same day great numbers of bull elk were reported, and also, "on some rugged hills to the southeast," numerous bighorn.

In all the records of western exploration and travel I can recall nothing that suggested such an astonishing plenitude of many kinds of large animals in one region. It would not have been so hard to conjure up the picture along some of the wilder reaches of the upper river, but here—with those pretty little forty and fifty-acre farms, all under ditch and cultivated to their last foot, stretching away mile after mile on my left—it was asking almost too much of the imagination to perform such acrobatics.

In a steady but ever slackening current it took me about four hours to pull the thirty miles to the Intake dam. The town was on the left but the abrupt bluff at that point indicated the right as the easier portage. The smooth green current of the water over the end of the concrete barrier tempted me for a moment to avoid portaging by letting down the empty boat on a line. Sober second thought counselled caution—that water at the end of a twelve-foot drop had too much of a kick in reserve to make it safe to trifle with. Better safe than submerged is a serviceable variation of the old saw for river use.

There was a considerable stretch of rip-raping and other rocky barriers—laid to protect the end of the dam at flood time—to get the boat over, but a young rancher, just driving up to the ferry, kindly volunteered to come up and give me a hand. Carrying the trim little craft bodily for a couple of hundred feet, we put it into his wagon and drove down a hundred yards to the ferry-landing where it was easier launching than near the dam. He was all against being paid for his trouble, but finally suggested twenty-five cents as his idea of what was fair. He looked actually distressed when, with a wristy movie actor's gesture of finality, I gave him the whole of a dollar bill. What wouldn't a farmer on a country highway have charged for half that much labour pulling a Ford out of a mud-hole?

But it appears that even non-river dwelling folk are not mercenary in this neck of Montana. A cowboy-like girl who had just ridden up on a prancing pinto frowned darkly when she saw the greenback pass. Spurring down to the water as I finished trimming the boat, she leaned down close to my ear, whispering stagily through her hollowed gauntlet: "Too bad you didn't see me first, stranger; I'd 'a yanked down that lil' sardine-tin there on the end of my rope for nothin'." That was the first time I ever heard anybody called "stranger" outside of Wild West stories written in the Tame East. Later, down Nebraska and Missouri-way, however, I found that address in common use by people in real life. There's no end of a thrill in finding story-book stuff in real life—I suppose because it happens so darn'd seldom.

There were a few flashes of white in the riffle below the dam; then a broadening river and slackening water. Many and unmistakable signs told me that I was now skirting the dread "Mosquito Coast." Cattle nose-deep in the water or rushing blindly through the thorny bull-berry bushes, smudge-barrages round the ranch houses, dark, shifting clouds over the marshes and over-flow lakes—every one of them was a sign of an ancient enemy, an enemy who had drawn first and last blood on every field I had met him from the Amazon to Alaska. Knowing that I was going to run the gauntlet of him for many hundreds of miles, I had come prepared, both mentally and physically. Nevertheless I looked forward with no small apprehension to a contest which could not be other than a losing one—for me. Moreover, I had too many dormant

147

malarial germs in my once-fever thinned blood to care to risk their being driven to the warpath again by too intimate contact with other Bolsheviki of the same breed. Frankly, Herr Mosquito, with his shrecklichkeit, was one thing above all others that had given me pause in planning a voyage that would carry me through so many thousand miles of his Happy Hunting Grounds. Miles and Terry and Crook had driven the Redskin from the Yellowstone and Missouri, Civilization had exterminated the buffalo, but the mosquito still ranged unchecked over his ancient domain. It was just a question of how much blood one was going to have to yield up to get by his toll-gate-keepers.

Some kind of a poor old river-rat—doubtless an agate-hunter,—ringed with smudges and trying to spare time enough from fighting the enemy to hold a frying pan over a smouldering fire gave me a graphic warning of what fate awaited me if I tried to camp by the bank. Forthwith I decided to get my supper in the boat, run till near dark, pick the likeliest-looking ranch, tell them I was a farmer myself, and let human nature take its course. I had had the plan of adding a galley to the boat in mind for some days. Drifting while I munched a cold lunch had already eliminated the noonday halt, and I was now figuring to let the river also go on with its work during breakfast and supper hours as well. My first plan was to make a little stove by cutting holes in an oil-can, setting this on the non-inflammable steel bottom of my boat and cooking with wood in the ordinary way. Then, in a store window in Glendive, I saw a midget of a stove that worked with gasoline pumped under pressure. It was called a "Kampkook," but I could see every reason why it would also make a perfectly good "Boatkook." Drifting just beyond the wall of the coastwise mosquito barrage, I tried it out that evening. Bacon and eggs, petit pois, mulligatawny soup, dried apricots and a pot of cocoa—all these delectables I fried, boiled or stewed without pausing from rowing for more than an occasional prod, stir or shake. When all was ready, I removed the thwart from the forward section, threw my half-inflated sleeping-bag in the bottom, disposed a couple of cushions, and suppered like Cleopatra on her barge, reclining at my ease. With occasional spice-lending-variations, that sybaritic program was followed on many another evening right on to the finish of my voyage. I loved too well the smell of "wood smoke at twilight" to forego entirely the joy of the camp on the bank, but wherever that

bank was muddy or infested by mosquitos, I. W. W.'s, or other unde-
sirables, or whenever I was trying to make time, I had a perfectly self-
contained ship aboard which I could eat and sleep with entire comfort.

It was early twilight before I came to just the ranch that I was looking for. Distantly at first, like the gold at the end of a rainbow, I saw it
transfigured in the sunset glow at the end of the vista of a long wine-
dark side-channel. There was a sprawling, broad-eaved bungalow,
vine-covered and inviting, big new red barns and a lofty silo that
loomed like a tower against the sun-flushed western sky. I named it
"Ranch of the Heart's Desire" on the instant, for I knew that it could
give all that I most intensely craved—cover from the enemy. I tied up
at the landing as a sea-worn skipper drops his anchor in a harbour of
the Islands of the Blest.

The long avenue of cottonwoods up to the bungalow seemed to be
filled with about equal parts of mosquitos and Jersey cows. Doubtless
the mosquitos were much the more numerous. But because it hurts
more to hit a running cow than a flying insect I probably was impressed
with the Jerseys out of all proportion to their actual numbers. A dash
through a "No-Man's-Land" of smouldering smudges and I burst into a
Haven of Refuge at the bungalow door. A genial chap with a steady
smile met me as I emerged from the smoke, complimented me upon the
smartness of my open-field running among the Jerseys, and opined that
I must have been a pretty shifty fullback in my day. A youth in greasy
overalls who came wiggling out from under a Ford he introduced as
"My hired man." But when the latter blushed and protested: "Now there
you go again, dear!" he admitted that it was only his wife. They
promptly insisted I should have supper, while I had considerable difficulty in making them believe I had a galley functioning in my boat. We
finally compromised on ice-cream and strawberries. All the ranchers
along the lower Yellowstone and upper Missouri have ice-houses.

They were just the kind of folk one knew he would have to find in
a haven called "Ranch of the Heart's Desire." Their name was Patterson, and they had lived most of their lives in Washington—in some
kind of departmental service. Becoming tired—or perhaps ashamed—
of working six hours a day, they bought a ranch under the Yellowstone
project ditch and started working sixteen. So far they had been spending rather more money than they had made but, like all on the threshold
of bucolic life, looked confidently to a future rainbow-bright with

prospects. They confessed that it awakened a wee bit of nostalgia to meet one who had been in Washington, and so it chanced that it was of "Things Washingtonese" that we talked rather than of our experiences as farmers.

There was something strangely appealing to the imagination in sitting there where the bison in his millions had so lately trod and putting everything and everybody at the Primal Fount in their proper places. Long into the night we rattled on just as though over a table at the Shoreham, the New Williard or Chevy Chase—just as we would have talked in Washington. Knocking Wilson whenever any other subject was exhausted, we bemoaned the predominance of third-class men in Congress, agreed that Harding wouldn't do much harm and might do good, swapped yarns about the funny things Congressmen's wives had said and done, and passed by acclamation a motion that the most un-representative institution in America was the House of Representatives. It was highly refreshing to meet people you could be really frank with in discussing the more or less esoteric phases of these and kindred subjects. I enjoyed that evening's yarn only less than I did my couch on a breeze-swept porch that was armoured with a woven copper mesh against the assaults of the common enemy.

Before I pushed off in the morning Mr. Patterson took me around two sides of his ranch and showed me some splendid fields of alfalfa and sweet clover, just ready for cutting. Prices were good, he said, and the prospects were bright for the best clean-up they had known so far. I have often wondered just how those green, fragrant fields looked ten hours later, just how much those optimistic forecasts were modified as a consequence of certain little inequalities of atmospheric pressure that were already making their differences felt in a lightning-shot murkiness hanging low on the northeastern horizon. I did not make sure of the Patterson's address and a postcard of inquiry I subsequently dispatched brought no reply.

I was aware of the heavy humidity of the atmosphere the moment I pulled out in the slow current of the still broadening river. There was plenty of air stirring but with no fixed plan of action in its mind. Now it would swoop down over the banks in sudden gusts; now it would blow down river for a few moments and then turn on its heel and come breezing right back, like a commuter who has forgotten his ticket; now it would deliberately "Box-the-Compass" right round the boat, as a cat circles a rat that it is just a bit chary about springing on.

The easterly gusts paved the surface of the water with evanescent patches of floating grasshoppers, evidently part of a flight that had not yet found lodgment in the growing fields under the irrigation project on the other bank. After each gust the fish would rise greedily to the feast for a few minutes. Satiation would come quickly, however, and most of the hoppers were left to drown or perhaps to gain a few hours longer lease on life by drifting to a bar. One gust that came while I was skirting the shore poured a literal grasshopper cataract over the cut-bank into the boat. There was a sharp, rasping contact where the saw-toothed legs side-swiped my arms and face that would undoubtedly have left abrasions on the skin if it had been kept up for any time. For a few moments there was a layer of hoppers two or three inches deep in the bottom of the skiff; then the most of them hurdled out into the water. The dessicated remains of the few ambuscados that took refuge in the grub-box kept turning up in a variety of frys, stews, and fricassees for the next fortnight.

I pulled up to Riverview Ferry, well on toward the North Dakota line, at one o'clock. Mr. and Mrs. Meadows, with whom I had lunch, once operated a pontoon bridge at this point but had given it up on account of the trouble from high water. They wanted to sell the twenty or more pontoons left on their hands but said they could not see where a buyer would come from. It occurred to me that one of these floats would make an ideal hull for a houseboat, for a Missouri-Mississippi voyage, just as Riverview would be an ideal place for launching one. I have not Mr. Meadows' address, but fancy Sidney, Montana, would reach him. I shall not take the responsibility of urging any one to attempt a trip of this kind, but should the urge have developed spontaneously I think there is a chance here to acquire the makings of an extremely serviceable house-boat at a fraction of what it would cost to go about building it in the ordinary way. Starting at high water in June, an outfit of this kind—with luck and in the hands of the right party—might well go through to New Orleans before Christmas. Manned by a party without much common sense and persistence, it might conceivably be abandoned by some wildly regretful people before it swung out into the "Big Muddy." I utterly refuse to pass upon any one's qualification, or to take other than hostile notice of letters

151

charging me with ruining what but for me might have been a comparatively inexpensive and enjoyable holiday in Bermuda or on the Riviera.

The ferryman at Riverview claimed to have made the voyage from Miles City to somewhere on the lower Mississippi in a house-boat, taking two seasons for it. He was the first ferryman I ever met who was full of doleful warnings about troubles ahead. My little tin boat might be all right for the rapids of the Yellowstone, he said, but just wait till it went up against the white caps kicked up by the winds of the Missouri and the Mississippi. He said no word about the winds of the Yellowstone. If he wasn't prepared for them, I only hope his ferryboat was not caught in midstream by a zephyr that breezed up river about three hours later.

It must have been toward three o'clock that I first noticed how what had been a grey murkiness to the north-east all morning was now rising in a solid bank of swiftly advancing cloud. For a while its front was smooth and rounded, like the rim of a tin-plate. Half-way up to the zenith this front began to reveal itself as a wind-riven line of madly racing nimbus, black, sinister and ominous. And yet, blissfully ignorant of the hell-broth a-brew, I worried not a whit—didn't even begin to edge away from mid-channel for a while, in fact. What a lamb it was! Never again, with so much as a man's-hand-sized cloud blinking on the windward horizon, was I to know the calm, quiet, serenity of a confident soul.

A long, lean, torpedo-like shaft of blue-black cloud, breaking away from the ruck and aiming in a direction that would bring it directly over my head, produced the first splash in the pool of my perfect serenity. That did look just a bit as though I might be running into the centre of a heavy thunder-storm, I confessed to myself. Perhaps, if there was a ranch-house convenient, it might be just as well to be thinking of getting under cover. Yes, there were three or four houses off to the left— places on the irrigation project, doubtless, they were so close together. I started to pull in toward a sandy flat, but sheered off again when it became apparent that a slough and marsh would cut me off from the first of the houses, a place with a silo and the inevitable red barn. Plainly the only way to reach any of the farms would be by landing at the foot of the bluff a quarter of a mile ahead, climbing up and cutting across the fields. That might not be possible before the storm broke— but what did a warm summer rain matter anyhow?

Leaning hard onto my oars, I headed straight down stream for where a coal-streaked yellow bluff blocked the northerly course of the river and bent it off almost directly eastward. Swelling monstrously as it approached, the black arrow-head of the storm, deflecting slightly, began to pass overhead to the left. I distinctly remember thinking how its shape now suggested the picked skeleton of a gigantic mackerel—just a backbone and right-angling ribs. The sun dimmed and reddened as the flying clouds began to drive across its face, and the even ribs barred the dulling glow like a furnace grating. A sulphurous, copperly glare streaming through cast a weird unearthly sheen on the unrhythmically lapping wavelets of the river. My serenity was blotted out with the sun. I recalled only too well now where I had known that ghostly yellow light before—the sullen fore-glow by which the South Sea hurricane slunk upon its helpless prey. It had always been associated in my mind with the shriek of the wind, the roar of the surf and the explosive detonations of snapped coco palm boles. There were no coco palms here to snap, I reflected, but—ah, that was surely a roar, and there came the wind!

Pulling in a dead calm myself, I saw the river and air at the bend turn white almost between one stroke and the next. A tongue of wind seemed to have shot out from behind a point to the right and begun scooping up hunks of the river and throwing them across the flats. This blast was at right angles to my course down stream, but I came parallel to it as I swung and headed for the sand-bar on my left. The air was coiling and twisting upon itself as I landed, but that out-licking tongue of the storm was passing me by and circling the bluffs beyond the flat.

Without unloading the skiff, I dragged her as far in on the bar as I could, threw my stuff together in the forward section and snugged it down under a tarpaulin. Its weight might keep the boat from blowing away, I figured. Then I drove oars in the sand with an ax and ran lines to them from bow and stern—land-moorings, so to speak. The forefront of the wind hard and solid as the side of a moving barn, caught me from behind as I made fast the bowline. I went forward to my knees, sprawled flat, wiggled round head-on and then, leaning far forward, slowly struggled to my feet. Hanging balanced at angle of forty-five degrees, I started slowly crabbing back to the boat. It wasn't so bad after all, I told myself. The skiff was not giving an inch to the blast, while leaning up against the wind that way was rather good fun. I recalled a stunt something like it that Little Tich used to pull in the London Halls—an eccentric dance with enormously elongated shoes. I decided that perhaps I was even enjoying the diversion a bit. In half-pretended nonchalance I turned my head and cast a side-glance over toward the farmhouses back of the bluffs. That was the last move of even assumed nonchalance I was guilty of for some time.

That side-glance photographed three things on my memory: a grove of willows flattened almost against the earth by the wind, two women, with wondrously billowing skirts, crawling along the side of a house toward a door, and a flimsy unpainted outbuilding resolving into its component parts and pelting across a corral full of horses. Doubtless there was more animated action to be observed had I been spared another hundredth of a second or so to get a line on it. The three things mentioned were as far as I got when the hail opened up.

With the viciousness of spattering shrapnel that first salvo of frozen pellets raked me across the right cheek. The tingle of pain was astonishingly sharp, like that from the blow of a back-snapped thorn branch on an overgrown trail, and I was a bit surprised when an explorative finger revealed no trace of blood. Hunching my neck brought my face under cover, but the batteries of the storm had got my range now and there was a decided sting to the impact of those baby icebergs, even through my slicker and shirt. People are very prone to exaggerate about the size of hail-stones, so I shall endeavour to make a special effort to be conservative about these. They felt a lot bigger when they hit, of course, but as I examined heaps of them afterward the average size seemed to be about that of shrapnel or large marbles. There may have been hail-stones the size of hens' eggs, but no one who was ever exposed to them in the open can have lived to tell the tale. Men looking out through the bars of jail may have seen them and survived to make affidavits; most other authentic reports of egg-sized hail-stones will doubtless be pretty well confined to the minutes of coroners' juries. Indeed, I am inclined to think that a considerable crimp would have been put in my down-river schedule by the comparatively diminutive pellets I faced on this occasion but for the shelter I presently found for my head under the side of the skiff.

As the hail-stones, flying before the wind, were hurtling along almost horizontally, huddling under the lee bow of the skiff protected just about all of me but my feet. Even that was not good enough, however, for the impact of the blows on the tops of my toes left an extraordinary ache behind it—something that I could not contemplate standing for an indefinite number of murderous minutes. Clawing over the side for a canvas or poncho to buffer the worst of the barrage, my hand came in contact with the roll of my sleeping pocket. That gave me an idea. The wind, getting inside the hollow bag, nearly tore it from my hands as I started to unroll it, but once I got it smothered under me the rest was easy. With my legs inside of the bag and the uninflated rubber mattress between my feet and the hail-stones, about all I had to bother about seemed to be a wind strong enough to carry the boat away and me with it.

From the way things developed for the next couple of minutes this appeared to be just about what was going to happen, however. I cannot recall ever having felt more panicky in my life than when I saw that that fore-running tongue of wind, which had originally come charging round the bend from east, had now circled southward along the bluffs below the farmhouses and was heading straight back into the east again. That meant that I was now occupying the almost mathematical centre of the vortex of a real "twister"—that I was about to be rocked on the bosom of a fairly husky young cyclone. Something pronounced in the way of an uplift movement was inevitably due the moment that back-curving tongue of air lapped round to the place it started from.

A whimsical comparison flashed across my mind in watching through the crook of my fending arm the witch-dance of that circling blast. In some town up-river I had seen a movie of the Custer Massacre, at the climacteric moment of which the howling hordes of Gall and Rain-in-the-Face and Crazy-Horse whirled in a wide circle round their doomed victims, the mental agonies of which latter were shown in successive cut-ins of close-ups. Now I was once assured by a world-famous movie star that he always actually felt in his heart—to the very depths of his being—the emotion he was called on to register, was it murderous lust, ineffable virtue, mother-love or what-not. Very well. Assuming this to be true of all great movie actors, I have very grave doubt if any of that silver-screen last-stand battalion of Custer's felt any more real a pricking of the scalp in watching the closing circle of dancing Redskins than did I in waiting for that spinning blast of wind to decide whether or not it was going to stage a "Pick-me-up" party.

It is not quite clear in my mind even now why things in my immediate vicinity did not start to aviate. Several loosely built structures on the bluff went flying off like autumn leaves, and wind enough to blow boards into tree-tops would have at least sent my boat rolling if not skying. I am inclined to think, however, that the failure of any marked heliocoptic action to develop was due to a lack of pronounced opposition on the part of a bluffing turncoat of a southwesterly wind. The latter skirmished just long enough to turn in the vanguards of the main storm, but took to its heels the moment the thunderbolt phalanx was launched upon it. It was the advent of this Juggernaut that marked the end of my consecutive impressions. Primal Chaos simply clapped the lid down over me and kept it there for several aeons—fifteen minutes to be exact.

Although it was rapidly getting darker, I had still been able to see not a little of what was going on up to the moment the God of the Thunders uncorked his artillery; after that I simply heard and felt and grovelled in the sand. The big red silo was the last of the old workaday world I remember seeing before my horizon contracted from a quarter of a mile to a scant ten feet. (I don't recall that old Jim Bridger ever made anything shrink as fast and far as that, even with the astringent waters of Alum Creek.) The boat and I were lying in a grey-walled cocktailshaker and being churned up with flying sand, hail and jagged hunks of blown river water. At first the resultant mixture was milk-warm, but presently it became literally ice-cold, so that I shivered in it like a new-shorn lamb. (The warm water was that blown from the river. The subsequent chilling, as I figured out afterwards, was due to the hail banking up against the windward side of the skiff, finally filling the forward section of the latter and drifting right on over to congeal my cowering anatomy.)

The thunder did not come into action battery by battery after its wonted practice, but seemed to open up all of a sudden with a crashing barrage all along the line. Flashes and crashes were simultaneous. The light of the jagged bolts broadened the diameter of my bowl by not a foot. The solid grey walls simply glowed and dulled like a ground-glass bulb when its light is switched on and off. Not one clear-cut flash did I see in the whole bombardment.

I have always been a great believer in whistling to keep up ebbing courage; not necessarily a blowing of air through pursed lips, but any easy and spontaneous action to show nonchalance and sang froid in the face of danger. The particular practice which had always seemed to produce the best results was reciting stirring and appropriate poetry. "Spartacus to the Gladiators" and "Roll on thou deep and dark blue ocean, roll!" had steadied my faltering nerve in many crises. On this occasion it was when the boat broke loose from its moorings and started to roll over upon me that I began to feel the need of spiritual stiffening. I must have picked on Kipling because "The Song of the Red War Boat" had been running in my head for a day or two.

"Hearken, Thor of the Thunder! (I sputtered)
We are not here for a jest."
But that was altogether too obvious. I broke off and began again:
"The thunders bellow and clamour
The harm that they mean to do;
There goes Thor's own Hammer
Cracking the night in two!
Close! But the blow has missed her...."

But that was premature. Far from missing her, the blow had at last got a shoulder under the bottom of my poor little skiff and over she came! By Thor's grace she hung there, instead of going on rolling; but those fifteen or twenty gallons of slightly liquefied hail seemed to drain straight from the base of the North Pole. I tried to continue registering nonchalance and sang froid, but accomplished an only too literal rendition of the latter. I was still spitting sand and quavering "There goes Thor's own Hammer" when the walls of my hail-hole began to brighten and recede—and presently it was a warm, soft summer afternoon again. That three-mile-wide Juggernaut of Primal Chaos was rolling away straight across those verdant irrigated farms of the Yellowstone Project and leaving desolation in its wake. I only hope that it chastened the mendacious ferryman at Riverview and made a sharp right-angle bend round the Patterson farm above Savage.

It was a considerably altered world that met the owl-like blink of my still somewhat sand-filled eyes. The big red barn and the silo still loomed against the sky-line above the bluff, and most of the other houses and barns were still standing. All of the windmills had slipped out of the picture, however, and many lesser wooden structures. Trees were broken off or uprooted in all directions. But the strangest effect was from the practical disappearance of the thousands of acres of standing crops—beaten into the earth by the hail. There, I knew, lay the real tragedy of Thor's little field-day. Quite likely no human beings had been killed—but how many human hopes? The American public like to think and talk in millions. Very well. There went a natural mill that was grinding up corn and alfalfa and clover and wheat at the rate of a million dollar's worth a minute. Who said the mills of the gods grind slowly? Much as I was longing for the cheering propinquity of fellow creatures just at that moment, I hated the thought of intruding upon the blank despair that I knew had preceded me as a guest in the farmhouse beyond the big red barn.

Laying out a change of dry clothes from one of my water-proof bags, I stripped off my wet ones and freshened up with a plunge into the warm, invigorating current of the river. Thanks to the lightness and simplicity of my outfit, salvage operations were easily and expeditiously effected. The skiff had dumped itself in blowing over and was ready for launching as soon as it was tipped back. Most of my clothes were dry; most of my grub wet. The worst loss in the latter was the sentimental one of the residue of my California home-dried apricots. I didn't care much for the darn things myself, but the people along the river had proved dead keen for the succulent amber slabs. Moreover, it had always lent a pretty touch at parting to hand my host or hostess something produced on my own ranch, with perhaps a few words about how it had been picked, pitted, sulphured, dried and packed by Mexican señoritas—all young and dark-eyed and beautiful. That last had been especially effective in lone cow-camps. Yes, I was sorry to be compelled to give the last of those apricots away all at once to prevent their spoiling from dampness. I resolved to buy some more to replace them—for making up intimate little packets of parting—at the first opportunity.

The river had become its own quiet self again within a few moments, and I pulled through a slow current to the foot of the bluff at the bend, which appeared to be the only place one could land and avoid the mud-flats. The long sand-bar on which I had ridden out the storm had been scoured almost beyond recognition by the blown river waters. In a dozen places channels had been scoured straight through it to the slough behind, and the latter, greatly augmented both from the river and from the drainage from the heights above, was pouring a muddy torrent back into the mother stream at the bend. I saw that I was luckier than I had at first appreciated in not having had the bar dissolve beneath my feet.

Fully resolved, if no alternative cover offered, to tunnel into the bluff to avoid exposure to another of Thor's Juggernautic joy-rides, I landed on a jutting ledge of water-soaked lignite at the bend. Stacking up my outfit, I clapped the skiff down upon it, threw a few lashings over the whole, and climbed out up the bluff. With the fields themselves deep in water and liquid mud, I had to zigzag cross-country toward the nearest house by following the embankments of the irrigating ditches. Not a blade of grass was left standing. All that remained of alfalfa, oats and corn was a tangled green mat half covered with slowly melting hail-stones. Half-grown corn had not only been beaten flat, but the very stalks were crushed and shredded as if pounded by hammers.

There was only one cheering thing about that whole sodden field of desolation—millions on millions of mosquitos had been battered to death by the hail. Great masses of them, literally pulped, had been strained out of the water and collected against heaps of débris in the ditches. One could scoop them up by the double handfuls. How often had I bemoaned the fact that every mosquito around some swampy Alaskan or Guinanan camp of mine had not a single head so that I could sever it with one fell swoop of and ax or machete! That was too much to hope for, of course; but right here was a tolerably fair approach to it. I squeezed three or four fistfuls of those pulped tormentors through my fingers and felt appreciably less depressed.

Cut off by a deep-scoured drainage canal from a direct approach to the farm of the big red barn, I fared back for a quarter of a mile to a road and a bridge. Crossing the latter and wading through deep puddles, I came upon what I first took to be a deserted ranch. The corrals were down, the barn partially unroofed, and the windowless house was all but stripped of its shingles. There was a response to my knock, however, and I entered a half-wrecked kitchen to find three men sitting round a table. A lamp was burning on a wall-shelf, but its flickering flame barely threw a glow above the top of the opaquely smoked chimney.

The greeting I received was unconventional—even slightly disconcerting.

"Are you broke?" boomed the blunt query from a big chap with a hammer, evidently just through tacking a blanket over a window. His two companions took pipes from their mouths and hung on my answer as though it might be a matter of considerable importance.

"Not at all...." I began, intending to go on and assure them that, far from being the hobo I looked, I had money in my pocket and a large bag of California home-dried apricots to give away. But they waited only on my denial.

"All right. Move on!" they chorused to the accompaniment of stagy gestures. "This is no place for a man that ain't broke. We are. Went broke half an hour ago. Hailed out!" An old fellow with whiskers added the explanatory trimmings.

I gulped two or three times and was about to frame a minimum demand for an hour to dry my wet togs by the fire when the big chap strode over, clapped me jovially on the shoulder and forced me into a chair by the table.

"Don't mind our little joke, friend," he said with a ringing laugh. "Whatever there is left in this shack in the way of comfort is at your disposal for the night, or as long as you want to stay. Where did the storm catch you? Car stalled on the road, I suppose."

"Boat—on river—sand-bar," I replied between gulps from the mug of steaming black coffee the big fellow had poured me.

The three of them exchanged glances, first quizzical and then indicative of dawning comprehension. Finally they threw back their heads and guffawed louder than ever. I finished my coffee and gave them time to finish their laugh. Then I asked, in a slightly hurt tone I fear, just what joke they saw in being caught on a sand-bar by an embryonic cyclone. Perhaps if they had been there themselves....

That set them off again, and I had time to pour and empty another mug of coffee before one of them was sufficiently recovered to reply. The old boy with whiskers was the first to get his merriment under leash, and so it was he who explained: "That wasn't what tickled us; we was only laughin' 'cause youse was already drowned an' had a gang scoutin' for your dead body."

As that fell well within the compass of my own sense of humour, I joined the mirth party too, and the four of us laughed all together. It appeared that a gang of ditch-hands, before taking to cover, had seen a man pulling down stream into the teeth of the advancing storm. The last they saw of him he was trying to climb out on a sand-bar. The waves were all around him and he appeared to be at his last gasp. When the storm had blown by and they looked again, no trace remained of man nor boat. That was substantially the story the ditch-hands told in recruiting a posse to search for the body. If they had ventured out from cover five minutes sooner they would have seen just what had become of both man and boat, instead of having to have it explained to them by a trio of hilarious farmers who seemed to feel the need of something in the way of comic relief to take the edge off the tragedy of being "hailed out."

The big chap's name was Solberg. He was of Norwegian descent, extremely well educated, and had spent a number of years teaching in the schools of Minnesota. I was only too glad to accept his invitation to stay over-night and dry out, especially as the weather appeared to be far from settled. After calling in my search-party, I returned home with him and we spent the remaining hours of daylight boarding up windows, patching the roof and rendering first-aid generally to his wounded house. The plucky fellow was far from being crushed. He admitted that his crops were a total loss, that he was borrowed up to the limit with the bank, and that he didn't even see just how he was going to pay any of his debts. And yet—if he could only get hold of a bunch of sheep to fatten. Sheep were more in his line. Perhaps, in the long run, he would be all the better off for having to get back to them. Calling over his collie, he took the dog's head between his knees and asked him what he thought about it. The intelligent animal eyed his master seriously for a few moments and then wagged his tail approvingly. "'Shag' thinks it will be best to go back to sheep," pronounced Solberg. Then, musingly. "Yes, I reckon sheep's the answer."

After supper Solberg said that he was a good deal worried about his neighbours to the east—that they were harder hit than any one else, and in rather worse shape to stand it. A woman and kiddies didn't make it any easier when a man was hailed out. X—— had seemed pretty despondent when he had dropped in just after the storm. Talked rather wildly. Said he was through for good. Solberg hadn't been quite sure whether X—— had just meant he was through with farming, or something else. He was rather a moody chap at best.... Perhaps no harm would be done if we took a turn over that way....

The "neighbour to the east" turned out to be the big red barn and silo which, during the storm, had stood to me as the symbols of all that remained stable in the universe. A young woman opened the door of the staunch little farmhouse to us—a girl with a baby in her arms and a couple of youngsters fastened on her skirt. Her face was pretty—decidedly so, as I saw presently,—but at the moment I noticed that less than the courage it expressed. There was a well of tears behind her fine eyes, but I knew the shedding of them was going to be postponed indefinitely. Solberg, after directing a questioning look round the kitchen and sitting-room, asked bluntly where her husband was. With a nervous glance in my direction, she replied evasively that he was "outside walking round," adding that she had milked the cows and done the chores herself. With a keen and sympathetic glance of understanding, my friend turned on his heel and vanished into the darkness.

Never having seen any one hailed-out before, I was somewhat at a loss to know just what form my comforting ought to take. Finally, doubtless subconsciously inspired by "The Greatest Mother in the World" picture, I scooped up all the kiddies in sight and started to dandle them. I had always won approving nods for pulling that kind of a stunt, whether it was in a London Zeppelin raid or a drive of Armenian refugees at Trebizond. Even here it was sound—theoretically at least—for it gave the mother a chance to use her hands and apron to wipe dishes. Where it miscarried was on the practical side—the oldest boy would keep putting his hob-nailed boot in the baby's eye. But when I had cached the baby in its crib and gagged the other two with a handful of wet dried apricots, instinct came to my rescue and headed me off on the proper tack—sympathy stuff. That is, I told her my own troubles and led her to forget hers in sympathizing with them.

Sincerely and unfeignedly sorry as I was for these people, I was (momentarily) almost as sorry for myself before I came to the end of that tale of woe. I was a poor farmer from California. (Just how poor, and in how many senses of the word, I didn't confess.) Of all the farmers in the world, none had so many troubles as the California farmer. Take oranges, for example. If the buds escaped the frost probably the tiny green fruit would succumb to the "June Drop." If the latter was weathered, there were the black scale, the brown rot and the red spider lying in ambush, complicated by the probability of water shortage at the end of the summer. If the fruit ran that gauntlet and came to maturity, then there lurked the worst menace of all—the January frosts. And finally, if the ripe fruit survived the frost barrage and reached the packing-house, it was only to be pushed on into the "No Man's Land" of an overstocked market. No man lived with so many Damoclean swords suspended over him as the California orange grower—unless it was the California peach, prune, apricot, grape, nectarine or olive grower; or the walnut or almond grower; or the alfalfa, barley or wheat farmer; or the truck gardener.

I had been all of these, I said, and was just about to go on particularizing on the diseases and dangers threatening each crop, as I had done with the orange, when the rustle of a skirt caused me to raise my bowed head. There she was, a half-wiped pie-tin still in the bight of her apron, standing over me and looking down with tears a lot nearer to brimming than when we entered.

"And so you have had to come up to Montana looking for work?" she asked in a voice vibrant with sympathy. "What a shame it is we're all hailed-out round here, with no work in sight, and nothing to pay for it with if there was."

Having over-sailed the mark by a mile, I hastened to trim in canvas and beat back onto the course as originally charted. The last year or two in California hadn't been so bad, I admitted. I had even made quite a bit of money, so that this little river jaunt of mine on the Yellowstone was really almost in the nature of a pleasure trip. (Funny thing, but that river-pleasure-jaunt assertion was the only statement I made at which she seemed inclined to lift an eyebrow.) I had brought a few of my California home-dried apricots along, I continued. Perhaps they would enjoy a few for a change. That was the point I had been manœuvring to. Now I would play my comforter rôle.

Spreading the last of my bag of sticky slabs out before the fire, I started to tell how they were made. First there was the picking by men and the cutting and pitting by Mexican girls. She interrupted to ask what the girls were paid. I told her about fifteen cents a box, adding that some of the defter fingered of them often made three and four dollars a day. She sighed at that, and wished she had a chance to earn that much—sure and safe where the hail couldn't get it.

Solberg came in with her husband at this juncture. He was a good-looking young chap, well set up and with the right kind of an eye. There was no doubt of the depth of his discouragement and depression, but he was plainly too good stuff to sulk for long. He shook hands warmly enough, but there was a trace of bitterness in the smile with which he remarked that he was glad to see that I had survived the hail better than had his oats and corn. I rattled right on about the apricots, telling of the sulphuring, sunning, stacking, binning and packing, adding—in a convenient moment when the wife had stepped out to shake the tablecloth—that ever effective little capsule about the Mexican señoritas, all young, dark-eyed and beautiful. The good chap actually lifted his head and took a deep, shoulder-squaring breath at that. He relapsed again when I failed to develop the theme, but it was only temporary. Ten minutes later, with great inconsequentiality, I heard him asking his wife how she would like to go to California and work in the apricots. Then he went over, wound up the Victrola and put on "Smiles! Smiles! Smiles!" What a lot of latent good there was in those California home-dried apricots, I reflected as we splashed along homeward! Surely I must not fail to renew my supply at the next town.

As we were preparing to turn in for the night, I took Solberg to task for his remark earlier in the evening to the effect that a woman and kiddies didn't make it any easier for a man who had been hailed-out. "Don't you think," I asked, "that a plucky little woman like that comes in pretty handy to buffer the bumps in a time of trouble like this?" For the first and only time my host was guilty of sarcasm. "Well," he said with a cynical glint in his blue eye, "if I had been in your place down there on the sand-bar I daresay I would have been glad of almost anything to buffer the bumps of the hail-stones. As it is, I reckon I can do my own buffering."

Recognizing the familiar symptoms of an ancient but still unhealed wound, I thought the best thing I could do under the circumstances was to concentrate on blowing up my sleeping-bag and turning in. Funny how imagination works in a man who is much alone. Given a pin-prick over the heart, with ten years of solitude to brood over it, and he'll convince himself that the original wound was from nothing of less calibre than a "Big Bertha."

The next morning was bright and clear, with no signs of any menace lurking under the northeastern horizon. Solberg accompanied me across his ruined fields to my boat. His corn and oats, he admitted, were a total loss, but he thought there were signs that the tough, stringy stalks of the sweet clover had some vitality left in them. He seemed especially attached to this beautiful plant, calling it "The Friend of Man" and saying that he had experimented with several foods and drinks from it that promised well for human consumption. There was something particularly appealing to me in this fine, and bluff, if slightly eccentric, chap. I think it was his wholesomeness—the firmness with which he seemed to have his feet planted on the earth. One who has been attracted to the French peasant for his love of the land from which he draws his life will know what I mean.

I pushed off into a quiet current that was in strange contrast to the wind-torn welter of white I had seen at that bend the evening before. The air on the river was fairly drenched with the heavy odour of crushed vegetation, which seemed to have drained there from higher levels. This was pronounced at all times, but where I skirted fields of sweet clover there was a palpability to the perfume which suggested that one might almost gather it in his hands and allow it to pour through his fingers. In the Marquesas there is a little yellow-blossomed bush called the cassi, the pollen from which blows far to leeward before the South-east Trade. At times I have thought that I could detect the delicate odour of blown-cassi ten miles at sea, yet never even in kicking my way through a copse of the fragrant little bush have I been assailed with such a veritable flow of perfume as coiled and streamed about me as I drifted down toward the mouth of the Yellowstone that morning after the great hail-storm. Doubtless, indeed, the hail was responsible. Crushed and dying, the voiceless "Friend of Man" was chanting its "Swan Song" in the only medium at its command.

A couple of miles below the bend where the storm had caught me I passed into North Dakota at a point called the State Line Ferry. An hour later I ran under the bridge of a branch of the Great Northern. It was a fine, bold piece of construction, and it was in my mind at the time that its builder must be an outstanding man in his line. This surmise was vindicated a month later when I found him putting in the first piers of a bridge to span the Missouri at Yankton. Incidentally, some of his false-work got in the way of my skiff and all but dumped me out into the "Big Muddy."

Below Forsyth's Butte, last of the outstanding landmarks of the Yellowstone, the country on both sides began to smoothen and flatten out and offer less resistance to the spread of the river. The broad overflow flats offered an ideal breeding ground for mosquitos, recalling to me that a very large portion of Clark's journey of early August was devoted to telling of the mental and physical suffering inflicted upon the members of his party by the swarms of stinging pests they had encountered just above and below the mouth of the Yellowstone. From Clark's time down to the present this particular region has always been regarded as "The Dark and Bloody Ground of the Mosquito Coast of Dakota." I was resolved to put bars between myself and the enemy that night—if not the mosquito bars of a hotel room, then the mid-stream sand-bars of the Missouri.

A broad, sweeping curve to the left, a wide bend, and then an equally broad and sweeping curve to the right opened up a long vista with low, dry, rounded hills at the end of it. With a quick catch of breath I recognized the telegraph poles of the Great Northern Railway and the scattering buildings of Fort Buford—both beyond the Missouri. A swift run under a crumbling cut-bank on the left carried me past an out-reaching tongue of yellow clay and into a quiet, sluggish, dark-stained current that came meandering along from the west.

I have mentioned the quieter, calmer current in which I had been drifting below Glendive. So it had seemed after the tumultuous mountain torrent which I had run from Livingston to Billings; yet in comparison with this decorous bride from the west the Yellowstone came to its marriage bed like a raging lion. Or, to borrow an animal from the next cage in the zoo, the Missouri, in coming down to meet and mingle with the Yellowstone, fared much like the lady who went out to ride on the tiger. If I may paraphrase:

"I finished my ride with the Lady inside,
And the smile on the face of the Tiger,"

meaning the Yellowstone. Without even pausing to crouch for a spring, the tawny, impetuous feline on whose back I had ridden all the way down from the Rockies, simply rushed out upon the muddy lamb from the western plains and gobbled it up. Seven or eight weeks later I saw the latter do the same thing to the Mississippi—crowd it right over against the Illinois shore and gulp it down. And along toward the end of October I remember thinking how like the blonde beast of the Yellowstone was a ropy coil of tawny current I found undermining a levee in Louisiana. According to the maps I had been travelling for upwards of three thousand miles on the Missouri and Mississippi, but in fancy it was the tawny tiger of the Yellowstone that had carried me all the way from the borders of Wyoming to the tide-waters of the Gulf of Mexico.

THE END

Sitting Bull and Buffalo Bill, 1885

Made in the USA
Monee, IL
16 September 2024

65878074R00096